T0294185

SWITZERLAND'S
JURA CREST TRAIL

About the Author

Ali Rowsell is a full-time teacher who has worked internationally, in countries including Australia, South Korea and Switzerland. She specialises in the outdoors, in particular mountain walking, and is a freelance International Mountain Leader.

Based in Sussex, Ali continues to venture into Switzerland on a regular basis, to visit the Jura, a place very close to her heart. Having lived in the southern part of the Jura for some time, Ali is very familiar with the local area and enjoys summer and winter activities on the mountains around Lac du Joux in particular.

SWITZERLAND'S JURA CREST TRAIL

A TWO WEEK TREK FROM ZURICH TO GENEVA

by Ali Rowsell

JUNIPER HOUSE, MURLEY MOSS,
OXENHOLME ROAD, KENDAL, CUMBRIA LA9 7RL
www.cicerone.co.uk

© Ali Rowsell 2019
First edition 2019
ISBN: 978 1 85284 945 0

Printed in China on behalf of Latitude Press Ltd
A catalogue record for this book is available from the British Library.
All photographs are by the author unless otherwise stated.

Route mapping by Lovell Johns www.lovelljohns.com
Contains OpenStreetMap.org data © OpenStreetMap
contributors, CC-BY-SA. NASA relief data courtesy of ESRI

Updates to this Guide

While every effort is made by our authors to ensure the accuracy of guidebooks as they go to print, changes can occur during the lifetime of an edition. Any updates that we know of for this guide will be on the Cicerone website (www.cicerone.co.uk/945/updates), so please check before planning your trip. We also advise that you check information about such things as transport, accommodation and shops locally. Even rights of way can be altered over time.

The route maps in this guide are derived from publicly available data, databases and crowd-sourced data. As such they have not been through the detailed checking procedures that would generally be applied to a published map from an official mapping agency, although naturally we have reviewed them closely in the light of local knowledge as part of the preparation of this guide. There are other accommodation providers besides those mentioned in this guide: the suggestions listed here represent a selection of the more convenient options along the route.

We are always grateful for information about any discrepancies between a guidebook and the facts on the ground, sent by email to updates@cicerone.co.uk or by post to Cicerone, Juniper House, Murley Moss, Oxenholme Road, Kendal, LA9 7RL.

Register your book: To sign up to receive free updates, special offers and GPX files where available, register your book at www.cicerone.co.uk.

Front cover: On the ridge descending into Saint-Cergue (Stage 13)

CONTENTS

Acknowledgements

The process of writing a book such as this is a complex task, made far easier by a number of people who helped along the way. Many local Swiss, in town and on the trail, helped make my days in their country very special. Some patiently gave directions or passed on their knowledge of the local areas, some wanted to converse and practice their English, which brightened the days when walking alone. Ian, a fellow International Mountain Leader, in particular provided me with detailed in-country mountain information, alternative routes, local specialities and alternative camping locations. I would like to thank Clair, Sofie and Laura for joining me on many Jura rambles and for keeping me company and entertained along the route. Last but not least, I would like to thank those who inspired me to take on this venture: my aunt, Patsy, who enlightened me into the art of travel writing; my parents, Sue and Dick, alongside Lara for encouraging me to persevere and let others know about the places I am passionate about.

Mountain safety

Every mountain walk has its dangers, and those described in this guidebook are no exception. All who walk or climb in the mountains should recognise this and take responsibility for themselves and their companions along the way. The author and publisher have made every effort to ensure that the information contained in this guide was correct when it went to press, but, except for any liability that cannot be excluded by law, they cannot accept responsibility for any loss, injury or inconvenience sustained by any person using this book.

International distress signal *(emergency only)*
Six blasts on a whistle (and flashes with a torch after dark) spaced evenly for one minute, followed by a minute's pause. Repeat until an answer is received. The response is three signals per minute followed by a minute's pause.

Helicopter rescue
The following signals are used to communicate with a helicopter:

Help needed:
raise both arms
above head to
form a 'Y'

Help not needed:
raise one arm
above head, extend
other arm downward

Emergency telephone numbers
OCVS (Organisation Cantonale Valaisanne de Secours): tel 144

If telephoning from the UK the dialling code for Switzerland is 0041

Weather reports
tel 162 (in French, German or Italian), www.meteoschweiz.ch/en

Mountain rescue can be very expensive – be adequately insured.

ROUTE SUMMARY TABLE

Stage	Start	Time	Distance (km)	Total ascent (m)	Page
1	Dielsdorf	9hr 30min	30	1120	46
2	Neustalden	9hr	29	1170	58
3	Hauenstein	7hr	21	1000	67
4	Balsthal	6hr 30min	19	1250	77
5	Weissenstein	7hr 45min	24	800	85
6	Frinvillier	6hr 30min	18	1300	92
7	Chasseral	5hr 45min	19	680	99
8	Vue des Alpes	6hr 45min	22	760	105
9	Noiraigue	10hr 30min	32	1700	113
10	Sainte-Croix	7hr	24	850	123
11	Vallorbe	4hr 30min	12	820	133
12	Col du Mollendruz	5hr 30min	17	950	145
13	Col du Marchairuz	5hr	17	480	153
14	Saint-Cergue	6hr 45min	26	800	162
Total: Dielsdorf to Nyon		**98hr**	**310**	**13680**	

Symbols used on route maps

~	route
- - -	alternative route
(S)	start point
(F)	finish point
(SF)	start/finish point
	woodland
	urban areas
	international border
▬■▬	station/railway
▲	peak
● ●	town/village
↑	hotel, guesthouse or B&B
⇧	hostel, youth hostel or auberge
■	building
	restaurant, cafe, food or buvette
	bus stop/parking
✈	airport
⅄ ⏚	campsite/picnic area
	castle/museum/tourist information
)(	pass
✳	viewpoint
★	point of interest
⸸	antenna

Relief
in metres

1600–1800	
1400–1600	
1200–1400	
1000–1200	
800–1000	
600–800	
400–600	
200–400	
0–200	

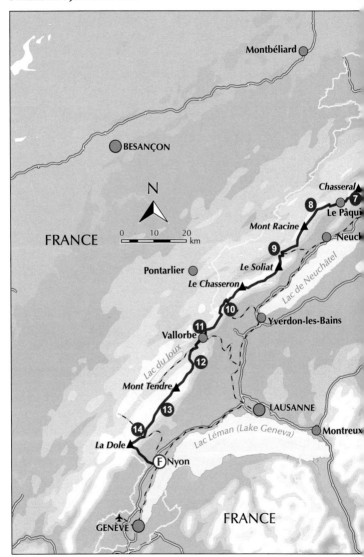

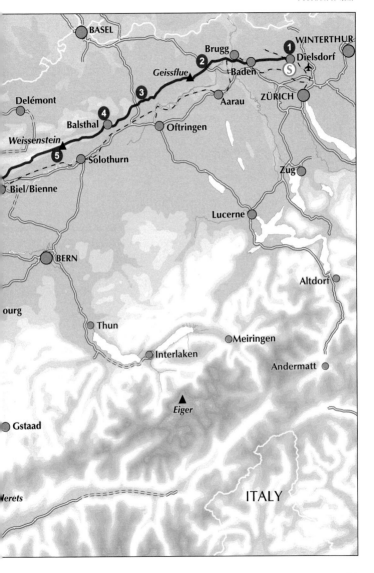

The end of the journey at Lake Geneva (Stage 14)

INTRODUCTION

View east from the highest peak of the range, Mont Tendre (Stage 12)

The Jura Crest Trail, one of seven Swiss national long-distance walking trails, delivers wondrous panoramas as you ascend, traverse and descend summits and mountain passes along the 310km trail. The day-to-day journey can be a challenge, with up to 1700m height gain in one day, but when you take in the immense views of the Jura range, the peaks and ridges of the Alps on the horizon, and across the Rhône valley, the sense of achievement more than compensates. Exertion apart, the trail does provide an enjoyable and relaxed trek as due to its location and access points, should you wish to, you can descend at any time.

That is, if you can pull yourself away. The route is a rolling showcase of natural features including deep gorges, mountain streams, glistening lakes (including the largest mountain lake in Switzerland above 1000m), tranquil forests, extensive alpine pastures and craggy exposed cliffs. A great pleasure of the Jura Crest Trail is derived from the many changes in its character as it moves from the north-east to the south-west. Throughout the Jura, nature reserves and protected areas are enforced to ensure wildlife and flowering plants are safeguarded. Made up of limestone, perfect growing conditions exist for a wide variety

INFORMATION AT A GLANCE

- **Currency:** Swiss Franc (CHF), although the euro is commonly accepted, especially at large hotels.

- **Formalities:** Western European and UK passport holders do not require a visa to enter Switzerland, whereas citizens of Canada, the USA, Australia and New Zealand can stay for up to three months without a visa.

- **Health precautions:** Healthcare in Switzerland is private, therefore expect to pay if you require treatment. It is important to be adequately insured. The European Health Insurance Card (EHIC) grants access to healthcare at a reduced cost, although it is possible that arrangements may change after the UK leaves the EU.

- **International dialling code:** Contacting Switzerland from the UK using a phone, dial 0041, ensuring you ignore the initial 0 on the remaining telephone number. Dialling a phone number in the UK from Switzerland is the same, except the dialling code is 0044.

- **Languages:** Two languages are spoken along the Jura Crest Trail: German from Stages 1–5, and French from Stages 6–14, although English is understood and spoken throughout.

- **Phones:** Phone boxes can be found throughout Switzerland, many of which are operated by phone card, which can be purchased at post offices, train stations and convenience stores.

- **Tourist information:** Switzerland Travel Centre is the main tourism company based in the UK, working directly with Switzerland Tourism and Swiss Federal Railways. See www.switzerlandtravelcentre.co.uk.

of flowering plants, and wildflowers are a particular point of interest here with over 950 flowering plant species.

THE JURA CREST TRAIL

The Jura Crest Trail, linking Zurich with Geneva, is also known as the Jura High Route (Swiss Route 5). At 310km in length and with over 13,500m of ascents on easy hiking paths, the trail requires a medium level of fitness. The route passes through two language regions – German and French – with the language border lying at Montagne de Romont (Stage 5); as the border divides cantons, the language merges and you will find some German-speaking on the French side and vice versa. The Jura Crest Trail interlinks through two cities along the route – Baden and Brugg – enabling access to a range of accommodation and transport to assist with the planning of your hike. Alongside mountain villages and passes, with bus routes and simple accommodation, there are also descents through small towns where provisions can be picked up on route.

The trail is regarded as the Swiss classic long-distance path, with waymarkers plotting the route as early as 1905, making the route fairly easy to navigate. Transport provisions at the beginning and end of the route are very good. The start point, Dielsdorf (15km from Zurich), and the finish point, Nyon (26km from Geneva), are both near to international airports and train stations that are connected with most countries in Europe. Regional trains are easily linked with local trains and post buses to provide widespread and regular transport from most of the start and finish points of each stage, as well as along the trail where small towns and mountain passes are crossed.

The Jura mountains form a range of ancient folded strata creating an arc from the Rhine valley in the north-east to the Rhône valley south-west, along the border between Switzerland and France. The word Jura originates from the Latin term *juria*, meaning 'forest'. The Jura has also been regarded as the Jurassic Alps because of the geological timescale in which they evolved. Characteristic of the Jura are combes,

Looking east towards the Lägern ridge from Baden (Stage 1)

Looking east along the Jura Crest Trail from the summit of Belchenflue (Stage 3)

sequences of geologic folds, dry valleys or depressions of limestone rolling and undulating along the high plateau. These relatively flat high-altitude features enable maximum access and enjoyment of the trail by all abilities and offer spectacular views across the Alps to the Rhône valley, the Black Forest, the Vosges and five lakes: Bielers, Lac de Neuchâtel, Lake Geneva (Lac Léman), Lac de Joux and Lac Brenet.

Beginning in the town of Dielsdorf, Stage 1 starts with navigating the cobbled streets of medieval Regensberg, a hilltop fortified village, before ascending and traversing a narrow, wooded ridgeline with intermittent views across to the Bernese Oberland. Towards the end of the Lägern ridge you approach the only mountain hiking graded part of the trail, involving the option of scrambling and descending a rocky ridgeline. Alternatively, the terrain to the northern side of the slope is an easier option to descend into Baden. The second half of the trail is wide and easy to walk, gently meandering through a variety of farmland, forest and passes through two large towns, Baden and Brugg, offering plentiful amenities, accommodation and transport options.

The route from Brugg to Balsthal, covering the end of Stage 1 through to Stage 3, is less densely populated, passing over several cols which link the trail with local towns via public transport. Accommodation along the route is good, although you are limited in what is available. The trail is mostly wide, passing through woodland and farmland, undulating along the Jura crest. The oldest tree in Switzerland, the famous 800-year-old linden tree is passed on the outskirts of the small village of Linn, as you traverse remote, rolling alpine pastures and forests. Several geological interest points can be found along the route, with exposed limestone crags at the end of escarpments, in particular on the geology trail near Hauenstein. Military history is evidenced throughout Stage 3, as you follow the World War I road carved into the mountain below Belchenflue. Remains of a hilltop fortress are passed, comprising small bunkers and outbuildings. Grubens, large hidden holes dug in an attempt to prevent tanks from entering Switzerland in World War II, alongside 'toblerone' tank traps and deeply sunk metal defences, can also be seen in the area. As you near the end of Stage 3, prominent geological features, such as the summit of the Roggenflue (995m), lead to a dramatic descent deep into the gorge at Balsthal, with commanding views of the upcoming Stage 4 ascent of 700m along the knife-edge Hällchöpfli summit.

Between Stages 4 and 5 from Balsthal to Frinvillier, over 30km of undulating ridgelines and high alpine pastures filled with wildflowers can be enjoyed. With a narrow, steep ascent from Balsthal winding its way up forested hillsides before opening onto rolling open alpine meadows en route to the Weissenstein, noticeable high points enable panoramic views alongside local access to other recreational activities such as a high-ropes course at Balmberg. The two stages remain high on the Jura, with several access points to local towns for amenities. This part of the Jura is popular with locals due to its access to well-maintained trails and good mountain restaurants. Nearing the end of Stage 5, the trail continues on wide farm paths and begins to become intermittently scattered with small chalets belonging to the local community. The trail then begins its gentle descent through the forest into Frinvillier.

Beginning close to the city of Biel/Bienne, Stages 6–8 involve a steep ascent from the Frinvillier gorge up to the prominent summit of Chasseral. From there, a remote, narrow path is followed along a rocky, forested ridgeline for most of the trail. The landscape changes noticeably as you approach the Tablettes and Noiraigue with their steep limestone karst and sheer drops, culminating in the spectacular amphitheatre of the Creux du Van. This region is famed for its absinthe, a highly alcoholic beverage becoming popular again, following the prohibition of it for many years. Along the route, there are opportunities to visit and sample the beverage in local buvettes, mountain hotels and museums.

Geological wonders can be found at the beginning of Stages 9, 10 and 11, where prominent summit peaks of the Creux du Van (1463m), Aiguille de Baulmes (1559m) and Dent de Vaulion (1483m) are passed before reaching landscape typical of the Jura: rolling high alpine meadows, forests and farmland pastures. The Creux du Van, sitting above the town of Noiraigue, is a perfect example of the Jura limestone seen at its best. The trail passes along the top of the impressive 160m-high vertical rock wall amphitheatre within a 1km-wide valley, offering stunning views of this geological formation. Aiguille de Baulmes, a sharp pinnacle of rock, is passed shortly after leaving Sainte-Croix, which sits within 600 metres with the border of France. World War

II relics are passed around the base, a reminder of how close Switzerland potentially could have been with enemy invasion. There is opportunity to explore 3km of underground caverns filled with stalactites and stalagmites in the Grottes de Vallorbe, just below the summit of Dent de Vaulion, at the start of Stage 11, near the town of Vallorbe.

Stage 11 begins with a long ascent from Vallorbe, to the summit of Dent de Vaulion (1483m). The trail travels from town, into farmland, alpine meadows and forest, before reaching the exposed and rocky outcrop of the summit. The Jurapark, a nature park that sits below the summit of Dent de Vaulion, is home to wolves and bears that have either been rescued or taken out of captivity. It lies just off

View over Lac du Joux and Dent de Vaulion (Stages 12 and 13)

route but is easily accessed along the footpaths in the area. From the summit, two options for descent are available: a narrow forest path to the car park Pétra Félix, which continues on to Stage 12, or an excursion to the small town of Le Pont. The settlement is situated on the shorefront of the highest mountain lake of the Jura, Lac du Joux, which is famed for its Vacherin Mont d'Or cheese museum and yellow gentian liqueur distillery. Campsites can be found around the lake, with the opportunity to also hire sailing boats or mountain bikes to circumnavigate the 10km^2 lake. The Vaudois Jura Park extends throughout the region from Stage 11 and the Dents de Vaulion to La Dôle in Stage 14, providing a protected area for wildlife.

The final stages provide some of the best scenery of the entire Jura Crest Trail. The highest peak of the entire Jura mountain range, Mont Tendre (1679m), can be found in Stage 12 between Col du Mollendruz and Col du Marchairuz. A prominent triangulation point can be found at the summit, leaving 360-degree panoramic views including views of the route ahead, along the rolling elevated plateau of the 'Balcon du Alpes'. The plateau from this stage to Nyon is interspersed with three high mountain passes connecting Lake Geneva with Lac du Joux through public transport such as Post Buses and the famous Little Red Train at Saint-Cergue.

Stage 13 continues along the plateau and passes the high point of Crêt de la Neuve (1495m) where access to an underground glacier can be located 1.5km east of the trail at Glacière de Saint-George. The Jura is famed for its dairy products, such as cheeses like gruyere, alpage and Vacherin Mont d'Or, and after going through rolling alpine meadows the route passes the legendary local cheese farm, Fromageriue des Fruitières de Nyon where you can sample regional produce. Saint-Cergue, a quintessential mountain village, is located at the end of Stage 13 providing extensive transportation links, a variety of accommodation and amenities, as well as its own ski resort.

Stage 14 begins with a gentle ascent through alpine pastures before reaching the spectacular geological formation of La Dôle (1677m) via a steep cliff face. The 'golf-ball' summit, as it is known locally, hosts several air traffic antennas, alongside the top of a ski run that descends into France. The final section of Stage 14 descends from the mountainous environment, into forest, farmland and vineyards, before reaching the final destination, Nyon. The Canton Vaud is famed for its production of white wines, alongside filet de perche, a fish speciality found in restaurants near the lake. With plentiful amenities, museums, castles and chateaus, alongside the inviting Lake Geneva in the summer months, Nyon provides the ultimate concluding location for a long-distance trail.

OTHER LONG-DISTANCE PATHS IN SWITZERLAND

Switzerland has a long-standing history with hiking paths, with the Jura Crest Trail (route 5) forming one of seven such well-established paths through the country. The other national routes are the Via Alpina (390km, route 1), the Trans Swiss Trail (500km, route 2), the Alpine Panorama Trail (520km, route 3), the Via Jacobi (445km, route 4), the Alpine Passes Trail (610km, route 6) and the Via Gottardo (320km, route 7).

Popular throughout Europe, the internationally recognised 12 'E-paths' link numerous countries across the continent, with the E4 following 239km of the Jura Crest Trail, from Saint-Cergue to Dielsdorf. The E4 traces a 12,000km path linking Tarifa in Spain with Larnaca in Cyprus to provide the longest path in Europe. The European long-distance paths are identified by a blue shield encircled by yellow stars with a letter 'E' and the number of the trail in the centre.

The summit of Chasseral (Stage 6)

GEOLOGY OF THE JURA MOUNTAINS

The Jura mountains are part of the Alpine foreland providing some of the oldest rocks in the Alps. The Jura began its development in the Jurassic period of the Mesozoic era, around 152 million years ago, when significant portions of Europe were covered by the Tethys Sea. Sediments became compressed on the ocean floor, forming rock: the abundant tropical marine life and fauna of this Mesozoic ocean can still be

GEOLOGIC PLACES OF INTEREST ALONG THE JURA CREST TRAIL

- **Mammoth Museum, Niederweningen** (Stage 1) – a museum dedicated to the discoveries of mammoth fossils in Switzerland and in particular the local area. This small but very informative museum slightly north of the trail, but easily accessible by public transport from Dielsdorf, Baden or Brugg, is worth the detour: www.mammutmuseum.ch.

- **Aargau Jurapark** (Stage 2) – a stepped landscape consisting of deep valleys, high mountains and the Jurassic plateau: www.jurapark-aargau.ch.

- **Thal Nature Park** (Stages 3 and 4) – a large nature reserve with stunning views of the expansive rolling hills of the Jura: www.naturparkthal.ch.

- **Chasseral Regional Park** (Stages 6 and 7) – a 400km² nature park with the Chasseral massif sitting prominently in the centre. Over 500 plant species can be seen, alongside geologic formations along the summit ridge: www.jurabernois.ch.

- **Creux du Van** (Stage 9) – a large, natural limestone amphitheatre above Noiraigue, also known as the Swiss equivalent of the Grand Canyon: www.myswitzerland.com/en-gb/creux-du-van-travers-valley.html.

- **Grottes de Vallorbe** (Stage 11) – over 3km of underground caves consisting of limestone stalagmites and stalactites close to the town of Vallorbe: www.grottesdevallorbe.ch.

- **Glacière de Saint George** (Stage 13) – a 22m-deep cave filled with a glacier that can be accessed and visited from mid-May to mid-November: www.nyon-tourisme.ch.

- **La Dôle** (Stage 14) – a 1677m summit atop of a dramatic geologic amphitheatre overlooking Lake Geneva and the Mont Blanc Massif.

witnessed today in the fossil-rich limestone of the Jura. In fact, it was in the Jura that rocks of this age – 'Jura limestone', named by the famous geologist, Alexander von Humboldt – were first studied.

The Cenozoic Era, over the past 65 million years, was when the main deformational thrust took place in the Jura. The oceanic floor was pushed upwards as tectonic plates collided, forming mountains. Several major thrusts and Alpine uplifts occurred to form the first Jura mountain around 35 million years ago.

As a result of Cenozoic orogeny and more recent erosion, fault lines, folds, anticlines, high plateaus, deep gorges and combes form the main topography of modern-day Jura. Due to the layers of limestone and marl, permeable rock surfaces have enabled underground water networks to develop, alongside natural features formed by erosion, such as craggy karsts and fissures.

WORLD WAR II AND THE JURA MOUNTAINS

The Jura mountains run parallel to the border with France and offered an escape route from Nazi-occupied territory during World War II. Visible fortifications, defences and remnants can be seen throughout the latter stages of the trail, in particular from Sainte-Croix to Nyon (Stages 10–14), where the Promenthouse Line (also known as the Toblerone Line), a defensive

Swiss 'toblerones', a frequent sight along the Jura Crest Trail and a reminder of recent Swiss military history

line of nearly 3000 tank traps, was built between 1936 to 1937 in preparation for the rise of armaments and potential invasion from Germany.

Just a few kilometres south-west of Sainte-Croix the number of World War II bunkers increases as the trail passes within 600 metres of the French border. Nearing the end of the stage, on the approach to Vallorbe, Fort de Pre-Giroud (www. pre-giroud.ch) is visible 2km to the south-east on the hillside as you follow the river L'Orbe. Built between 1937 and 1941 to protect the Franco–Swiss border and the Col de Jougne, this underground fortress, its entrance identified by a false chalet with a large Swiss cross, housed 200 men. Today it is open to visitors (English tours by advance appointment).

Stage 11 passes close to the Grand Risoux Forest in the Vallée de Joux. The forest presented the perfect natural border between occupied France and the freedom of Switzerland, offering an advantageous starting point for those wishing to flee from the Nazi occupation. Only a small 3ft-high drystone wall with Fleur-de-Lis decorating it separated the two countries, allowing Jews, allied service personnel and resistance fighters to enter neutral Switzerland.

In 1940 up to 15 locals from the Vallée de Joux joined the Swiss Information Service (SR), part of the Intelligence Services, to set up a small group of *passeurs*, also known as smugglers, to organise, supervise and guide safe passage through the 200km of forest trails. One member, Frederic Reymond, a watchmaker who worked alongside resistance fighters and spies without hesitation, received the Yad Vashem medal of the Righteous Among the Nations after the war ended. Some *passeurs*, such as Bernard Bouveret, were not so lucky. A local man from Chapelle-des-Bois, Bouveret worked with Reymond to transport confidential documents regarding Nazi movements and microfilm to the British Embassy in Lausanne, and armaments to resistance fighters over the border in France. He was captured in 1944 and spent the rest of his war years in the German concentration camp, Dachau. Several *passeurs* were shot on sight.

Locals Anne-Marie Piguet and Victoria Cordier worked together to transport German and Austrian Jewish orphans between Champagnole in France, through the Risoux Forest to the safety of Zurich during the last two years of the war. The journey for the orphans started at the Chateau de la Hille near Toulouse, 700km away.

Numerous routes were formed throughout the forest to prevent the Nazis from tracking the *passeurs* from the several garrisons near the border. Many of the routes can still be traced today. Locals would purposely make random routes in the snow and in the undergrowth to make it more difficult to monitor and control the passage of escapees. The Nazis patrolled the

French side of forest throughout the day and night, firing without warning if anyone was found within the 2km forbidden zone at the border.

Once over the border, the guided group would rest and recover from the long, difficult journey at one of two wooden huts deep in the forest: L'Hôtel d'Italie and Le Rendezvous des Sages. From here, the *passeurs* would turn back and return to their homes before dawn, leaving the escapees to continue the 10km journey from the border before they could register and remain in internment camps for illegal foreigners, within the safety of Switzerland.

More than 100 Swiss wartime activists were accused, fined or imprisoned for charging money and profiteering from smuggling during the war, despite the selfless bravery. *Passeurs* admitted to carrying contraband such as chocolate and cigarettes during their journeys, to keep the Nazis off the scent, as this only involved a fine, instead of being interned in a concentration camp or, worse still, instant death by shooting. It has only been since 2009 that the *passeurs* have officially been recognised.

Several memorials to them can be found in the Vallée de Joux. A metal plaque can be seen near the top of the rock-climbing route through the Gy de l'Echelle in the Grand Risoux Forest, commemorating the movement of Jewish orphans. In 2014, an official memorial was unveiled at Le Pont and at Chapelle-des-Bois to pay tribute to the *passeurs* of the Risoux.

For further information on the *passeurs*, visit www.lespasseursdememoire.ch or www.randodespasseurs.com.

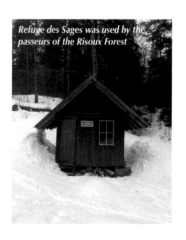

Refuge des Sages was used by the passeurs of the Risoux Forest

The Jura mountains are a haven for wildflowers due to the well-drained soils and other environmental conditions, and are home to over 950 flowering plant species. The Jura is made up of limestone, a sedimentary rock that offers the perfect growing conditions for a wide variety of flowering plants; in particular, the slopes and plateaus of the Jura from between 1000m and 1800m, where the grazing pastures are opened up to cattle in the summer and covered with snow

Top row (left to right): *Bladder campion; field scabious; yellow gentian.*
Bottom row (left to right): *alpine pasqueflower (seeded); plume knapweed; greater masterwort.*

in the winter. These areas suffer from relatively little agricultural chemical change, leaving natural meadows where a variety of species will flourish. Wildflowers appear as early as March and wilt away as late as October, depending on the year.

The best months to see the alpine meadows in their full beauty is between June and early August, when a range of colours scatter the hillsides, leaving scents of perfume lingering, which can be tasted in the local Alpage cheeses of the region.

Some of the wildflowers characteristic of the Swiss Jura include:

- **Yellow gentian** (*Gentiana lutea*), abundant in the Jura region and farmed and distilled in the Vallée de Joux to make a botanical liqueur drunk as a digestif
- **White hellebore** (*Veratum album*), a toxic plant that is a member of the lily family
- **Eyebright** (*Euphrasia officinalis*), a low-growing parasitic plant with white flowers, found in alpine pastures and grasslands

- **Monk's-hood** (*Aconitum variegatum*), also known as wolf's bane, a highly toxic plant with blue-violet flowers, found in mountainous terrain and rockier parts of the Jura
- **Field gentian** (*Gentianella campestris*), found in most alpine meadows, pastures and forest clearings throughout the Jura and identifiable by its four large blue-violet petals with a central corolla
- **Edelweiss** (*Leontopodium alpinum*), generally found high, on rocky outcrops or inaccessible areas
- **Harebell** (*Campanula rotundifolia*), a hardy and tolerant singular blue-violet nodding flower that is a member of the campanula 'bell' family
- **Grass of parnassus** (*Parnassia palustris*), distinguished by its white flowers with distinctive clusters of yellow stamens at the centre of the five petals and translucent green stripes atop of long stems with dark green heart-shaped leaves
- **Bladder campion** (*Silene vulgaris*), a flower with a pink bladder-like bulge and white petals clumped together in five bunches; its leaves are used throughout the Mediterranean in various food dishes such as gazpacho and omelettes
- **Alpine pasqueflower** (*Pulsatilla alpine*), a toxic plant bearing white-yellow flowers early in the season and distinctive seed heads atop of hairy, textured stems later in the year
- **Field scabious** (*Knautia arvensis*), a tall, hairy flower with pink anthers consisting of four unequal petal lobes that attracts butterflies, bees and insects
- **Carline thistle** (*Carlina vulgaris*), found on dry alpine pastures and identifiable by its clusters of spiky, brown-golden flower heads, not too unlike a thistle
- **Rosebay willow herb** (*Chamerion angustifolium*), a colonising plant also known as bombweed after it sprouted up in wasteland following World War I and World War II bombings throughout Europe
- **Greater masterwort** (*Astrantia major*), a member of the carrot family with a tall, hollow singular stem bearing an umbellifer head of flowers, that are very popular with butterflies
- **Plume knapweed** (*Centaurea uniflore*), easily recognisable by the straight stem covered with short rough hair and grey-green leaves of less than 1cm, and a pineapple bud under the thistle-like flowering head.

Protected areas

Throughout the Jura, there are a number of nature reserves and protected areas, identified by localised signage. These are in place to protect flowers and wildlife of the area, therefore should be respected. You should not pick any wildflowers, as they are unlikely to survive outside of their natural habitat. Some flowers, such as edelweiss, are protected throughout the Alps and could result in an offence being committed if you pick the flowers.

WHEN TO GO

It is important to choose the right time to walk the Jura Crest Trail, as snow can fall as late as April, and as early as October, leaving the highest parts of the trail hidden. This, alongside the high winds that sometimes cross Lake Geneva, can cause the wind chill to drop significantly. Do remember that the Jura rises up to 1679m in height. It is a mountainous area, providing microclimates that could rapidly cause adverse weather conditions as seen in the Alps, even though it is considerably lower than most of the mountainous regions of Switzerland. Close to the southern end of the Jura, Mouthe, 10km inside the French border, is regarded as the 'French Siberia' because its temperature dropped to -41ºC in 1985. The underground glacier in Saint-George (Stage 13) remains frozen year round, demonstrating the extreme temperatures that can occur on the Jura.

The best time to hike the Jura Crest Trail is between the months of May and September but do be aware that some mountain buvettes and hotels may not open until June, and potentially close at the end of August. Alpine flowers, such as crocus

View south from Dent de Vaulion (Stage 11)

Climate expectations – Baden (378m)				
May	7–17°C	62mm rainfall	11 rainy days	5 sunny days
June	10–20°C	60mm rainfall	11 rainy days	5 sunny days
July	12–23°C	63mm rainfall	12 rainy days	7 sunny days
August	12–23°C	58mm rainfall	10 rainy days	9 sunny days
September	9–20°C	59mm rainfall	9 rainy days	7 sunny days

Climate expectations – Mont Tendre (1679m)				
May	2–10°C	197mm rainfall	21 rainy days	4 sunny days
June	5–13°C	165mm rainfall	18 rainy days	5 sunny days
July	7–16°C	156mm rainfall	17 rainy days	7 sunny days
August	7–16°C	156mm rainfall	16 rainy days	8 sunny days
September	4–12°C	150mm rainfall	15 rainy days	7 sunny days

and spring gentians, can be seen as early as April on the Jura, depending on the winter temperatures and late snowfall. Wildflowers carpet the hillsides throughout most of the walking season.

Sudden storms can occur during August, as happens in the Alps, because of the moisture, the ground temperature and rapid rise of warm air, as well as microclimate developments such as weather movement across Lake Geneva. Also be aware that the temperature drops significantly at night during the summer months, so be prepared with warm clothing and be sufficiently equipped.

The maritime-continental climate of the Jura, alongside the height of mountain summits, means that annual precipitation increases as you travel south-west, with Mount Tendre having up to 2030mm of rainfall a year. On average, more heavy rain falls during the summer than in any other season, which is due to increased humidity, temperatures and the afternoon storms that develop in the Alps. For example, the pass over the Vue des Alpes (Stage 7) sees the most precipitation in the months of June to September, with monthly average rainfall of up to 120mm.

SUGGESTED ITINERARIES

The route is described in 14 stages (2 weeks), averaging 22km per day. Quicker or more relaxed itineraries are possible and suggested 12, 16 and 21-day schedules are set out here. It is possible to walk the whole route in a slightly shorter timeframe of 12 days, or over a slightly longer period, which would allow for shorter daily stages, optional rest days and more time for sightseeing in places of interest. The suggestions below can be adapted to suit your own individual requirements. In the option taking 16 days, Stages 11 and 12 could be combined to add an additional rest day. In the option taking 21 days, shorter walking

The Jura Crest Trail in 12 days

Stage		Time	Distance (km)	Total ascent (m)
1	Dielsdorf to Neustalden	9hr 30min	30	1120
2	Neustalden to Hauenstein	9hr	29	1170
3	Hauenstein to Berggasthof Schwengimatt	9hr 30min	26	1500
4	Berggasthof Schwengimatt to Grenchenberg	9hr	25	1220
5	Grenchenberg to Chasseral	10hr	31	1400
6	Chasseral to Vue des Alpes	5hr 40min	19	680
7	Vue des Alpes to Creux du Van	9hr	27	1450
8	Creux du Van to Sainte-Croix	7hr 50min	27	700
9	Sainte-Croix to Vallorbe	7hr	24	850
10	Vallorbe to Cab du Cunay	8hr	24	1430
11	Cab du Cunay to Saint-Cergue	6hr 30min	21	450
12	Saint-Cergue to Nyon	6hr 45min	26	800

The Jura Crest Trail in 16 days

Stage		Time	Distance (km)	Total ascent (m)
1	Dielsdorf to Brugg	7hr 30min	25	750
2	Brugg to Geissflue	8hr 30min	25	1200
3	Geissflue to Balsthal	9hr	30	1200
4	Balsthal to Weissenstein	6hr 30min	18	1250
5	Weissenstein to Frinvillier	7hr 45min	24	800
6	Frinvillier to Chasseral	6hr 25min	18	1300
7	Chasseral to Vue des Alpes	5hr 40min	19	680
8	Vue des Alpes to Noiraigue	6hr 45min	22	760

9	Noiraigue to Chasseron	8hr 45min	25	1500
10	Chasseron to Le Suchet	5hr	15	650
11	Le Suchet to Vallorbe	3hr 45min	13	100
12	Vallorbe to Le Pont	4hr	11	800
13	*Rest day: Le Pont*	–	–	–
14	Le Pont to Col du Marchairuz	7hr 30min	22	1230
15	Col du Marchairuz to Saint-Cergue	5hr	17	480
16	Saint-Cergue to Nyon	6hr 45min	26	800

The Jura Crest Trail in 21 days

Stage		Time	Distance (km)	Total ascent (m)
1	Dielsdorf to Baden	4hr	13	500
2	Baden to Brugg	3hr 20min	11	250
3	Brugg to Salhöhe	7hr	21	970
4	Salhöhe to Hauenstein	4hr	12	550
5	Hauenstein to Balsthal	7hr	21	1000
6	*Rest day: Balsthal*	–	–	–
7	Balsthal to Weissenstein	6hr 30min	18	1250
8	Weissenstein to Frinvillier	7hr 45min	24	800
9	*Rest day: Biel/Bienne*	–	–	–
10	Frinvilliar to Chasseral	6hr 25min	17	1300
11	Chasseral to Vue des Alpes	5hr 40min	20	680
12	Vue des Alpes to Noiraigue	6hr 45min	22	760
13	Noiraigue to Chasseron	8hr 45min	25	1500
14	Chasseron to Le Suchet	5hr	16	650
15	Le Suchet to Vallorbe	3hr 45min	14	100
16	*Rest day: Vallorbe*	–	–	–
17	Vallorbe to Le Pont	4hr	11	800
18	*Rest day: Le Pont*	–	–	–
19	Le Pont to Col du Marchairuz	7hr 30min	22	1230
20	Col du Marchairuz to Saint-Cergue	5hr	17	480
21	Saint-Cergue to Nyon	6hr 45min	26	800

The view towards Hauenstein is typical of the Jura landscape (Stage 2)

days at the start of the trek allow time to explore the historic spa town of Baden and picturesque Brugg.

Shortening the trek

Not everyone tempted by the Jura Crest Trail will be able to complete 14 days of walking. Presented below are suggestions for two shorter trips and a fortnight break, combining highlights of the route with local sightseeing excursions.

Walk 1: Dielsdorf to Brugg (Stages 1 and 2 over a long week-end) – Both the start and end location of these stages (finishing in Brugg, not Ursprung) are within easy reach of Zurich international airport and regional train lines; with minimal travelling times, there is more time available to enjoy the first stages of the Jura Crest Trail, and explore the city sights of Baden and Brugg.

Walk 2: Le Pont to Nyon (Stages 11–14 over one week) – With opportunities to spend an extra day at Le Pont you can enjoy a visit to the Grand Risoux Forest and learn about the *passeurs*, a tour of Vacherin Mont d'Or cheese museum at Les Charbonieres or a paddle on the lake, before summiting Dent de Vaulion and continuing Stage 11. At the end of Stage 14, spend an extra day in Nyon and explore the historic town and Lake Geneva.

Walk 3: Hauenstein to Le Pont (Stages 3–11 over two weeks)

– Following a day's travel, depart Hauenstein for a World War I and World War II historic first day. Continue Stages 4 and 5, taking a day of rest in Biel/Bienne, exploring the Frinvillier gorge. Start the steep ascent to Chasseral, continuing Stages 6–8 to Noiraigue, dropping off the trail to Neuchâtel to see the lake and old town. Continue on Stages 9–11, spending a day exploring Lac du Joux and the surrounding sights.

GETTING THERE AND AROUND

By air

There are two main Swiss international airports: Zurich and Geneva, both of which have numerous scheduled flights daily from most UK and European airports. Zurich is the nearest airport to the start of the Jura Crest Trail, although a return flight to Geneva may be the better option to minimise costs and open more options in terms of flight times and locations to travel between. Both airports are accessible by public transport, in particular main line train stations, from almost anywhere in Switzerland.

The flight time between London and both Swiss airports is one hour 40 minutes. The main carriers that provide flights between the UK and Zurich are: British Airways (www.british airways.com), SWISS (www.swiss. com), Easyjet (www.easyjet.com) and Edelweiss Air (www.flyedelweiss. com). Over 24 European airlines fly

The start of the 750m ascent from Balsthal train station (Stage 4)

into Zurich from a range of destinations, alongside international flights to over 62 countries worldwide. Carriers flying between the UK and Geneva include: British Airways, SWISS, Easyjet, Flybe (www.flybe.com), Jet2 (www.jet2.com) and TUI (www.tui.co.uk). Over 55 international airlines from around the world fly into Geneva airport, making it an accessible transport hub for the Jura Crest Trail.

From Zurich Airport, you can either take the bus or the train, travelling to the start of the route in Dielsdorf within 30 minutes of leaving the airport. With only one connection, if you time it right, you can travel by train between Geneva Airport and Dielsdorf in just three hours 40 minutes, changing at Zurich.

From Nyon, Geneva Airport is only 25 minutes away on the fast, direct train, and up to 33 minutes away on the regional, changing onto the connecting train at Geneva. To travel back to Zurich Airport from Nyon, the journey will take three hours, with one connection, changing at Zurich.

By rail

Eurostar (www.eurostar.com) and TGV (https://en.oui.sncf/en/tgv) make it surprisingly easy to travel between London and Zurich by train in seven hours 30 minutes, via Paris Gare du Nord. The Eurostar departs London St Pancras up to six times daily during the week and up to four times daily at weekends. Taking the TGV and

Eurostar back to London from Geneva is under seven hours in duration, via Paris, leaving Switzerland up to seven times daily on a weekday, and up to four times daily on a weekend.

Please note that Eurostar operate the trains under the English Channel, between London and Paris Gare du Nord and TGV operate the trains from the Gare de Lyon and Switzerland, therefore it is necessary to transfer upon arrival. There is a direct Metro line between the railway stations taking approximately 35 minutes costing €2, or alternatively a taxi can be taken which takes approximately 25 minutes in typical daytime traffic and costs about €25.

SwissPass Half-Fare travelcard

For discount travel throughout Switzerland, making use of trains, buses, boats and mountain railways, purchase the SwissPass Half-Fare travelcard for 120 CHF. You can purchase it online or at the train station, although you must have a passport photo and identification with you. The pass lasts for one month, therefore if you are undertaking long journeys, for example from Geneva airport to Dielsdorf, it may be worth purchasing it.

Intermediary access

Access to the Jura Crest Trail is frequent and reliable due to the extensive public transport system in Switzerland. The topography of the Jura leads to regular undulating features such as cols, which provide good access to the trail. Details can be found in stage information boxes at the start of each section of the trail.

ACCOMMODATION

Generally the stages have several options to choose from, enabling the hiker to select the most appropriate to their needs. With the Jura Crest Trail being close to civilisation, there is always accommodation available. Unfortunately, this is not always accessible on the route, and instead you may be required to travel into a local town. This is also true of budget accommodation, whereby mountain hotels may be accessible upon a summit, but at a costly price; a hostel or campsite off the mountain completely is often much cheaper.

Outline details and suggestions are provided throughout the guide where accommodation exists. These are also provided in Appendix A. Contact details such as telephone numbers and email addresses have been provided, as booking ahead is recommended. The Jura is busy during July and August and accommodation must be reserved in advance. Outside of these months, some lodgings shut completely, opening only if booked in advance.

On average, hotel prices in Switzerland compare reasonably to the UK and provide good quality accommodation and amenities for the night. Dormitories in mountain

A typical CAS hut sleeping area

huts and hotels provide the cheapest accommodation along the route, although can sometimes be quite basic, involving rooms laid with mattresses. Throughout the Jura Crest Trail, Club Alpine Suisse (CAS) huts are available as cheaper options to hotels. The Swiss Alpine Club is a well-established and prestigious organisation that promotes mountain sports. Basic dormitories are provided at a discount for members, alongside a kitchen area for the self-sufficient backpacker. The dormitory rooms must be booked in advance to ensure you have access, as they are not always manned. Another basic type of accommodation found in several places along the route is 'sleeping on straw' (*schlaf im stroh*), whereby you bring your own sleeping bag and enjoy a night in a barn. This traditional type of lodging is popular and enjoyable. Camping is an option along the route in designated campsites. Off-site or wild camping is officially prohibited in Switzerland, but if you are discreet and pitched off the route, away from habitation, a single night should not be an issue.

FOOD AND DRINK

The mountain restaurants and *buvettes* in the Jura are popular with both hikers and locals, as most have vehicular access and parking spaces. The term 'buvette' derives from ancient French and translates as a small refreshment room or bar where drinks and snacks are sold. Popular throughout the Jura, these small farm buildings, which are occupied for several months of the year, in particular from June to August offer a selection of beverages and meals for the hiker. In recent years, they have become quite fashionable, with some providing an outdoor restaurant serving specialities such as fondue, *rösti*, *croûtes*, and local meat and cheese dishes.

Throughout the Jura Crest Trail there are ample buvettes to provide a substantial meal during the day, although, as with most restaurants in Switzerland, these can be expensive. Some sections have a limited number of restaurants and buvettes to choose from, such as Stage 2 between Linn and Hauenstein and Stage 6 between Frinvillier and Chasseral, but the

A typical rösti served in most buvettes in the Jura

route descriptions list those that are available.

Most dishes are based on meat, cheese and bread products and vegetarians are catered for. Some local specialities include:

- **Rösti:** a traditional grated potato fritter dish, originally from the canton of Bern. It is served with your choice of accompaniments from mushrooms and fried eggs, to local cheeses and hams.

- **Croûte au fromage:** a bread-base, toasted and smeared with garlic and brandy, heaped with melted Alpage cheese (local to the area) and baked in an oven. Most buvettes offer additional ingredients such as a slice of local farm ham, a fried egg or mushrooms.

- **Fondue:** usually served *moitié-moitié*, meaning half and half (of two cheeses), making use of local cheeses of the area. The dish is always served with rustic bread, and can be accompanied with a plate of local cured meats. Alternatively for meat-lovers, *fondue bourguignonne* can be found in some buvettes. Instead of a dish of melted cheese, hot oil is provided for meat to be cooked in to your liking.

- **Raclette:** a semi-soft cheese that is melted on small pans over a stove, served with whole baby potatoes, *cornichons* (small pickled gherkins) and silverskin onions.

- **Vacherin Mont d'Or:** a seasonal (September to April) rich and creamy cheese found in the latter stages of the Jura Crest Trail, in particular throughout the Vallée de Joux. Produced and stored in circular pine boxes made from the Jura forests, the dish is pierced and stuffed with garlic cloves and drizzled with a glass of white wine before being baked in an oven. The dish is served over crushed whole baby potatoes.

Self-catering is a possibility, and provisions are generally quite accessible. This is especially true through stages that pass large conurbations, such as Stage 1 where the towns of Baden and Brugg offer plentiful opportunities. Despite the trail following the high Jura plateau, it passes over cols with public transport, alongside farm roads every few kilometres, enabling access to local towns, facilities such as farm shops, markets and convenience stores, and provisions.

The stages have been organised to start and finish at locations with good access to public transport or amenities such as cols or villages, to assist the independent, self-catering hiker. Some stages have limited provisions along the route, such as between Stages 2 and 3, where only a simple farmers' market is available in the village of Hauenstein, and between Stages 4 and 5 where basic provisions can be purchased from buvettes and farms. Planning ahead is sometimes required if you choose to self-cater during the early stages.

LANGUAGE

Switzerland officially has four main languages: German, French, Italian and Romansh, with German being the most spoken language throughout the country. German is spoken for the first six stages of the Jura Crest Trail; French is spoken for the remaining eight stages. English is widely understood and spoken throughout the route, and will almost certainly be spoken by staff at lodgings, resorts and larger towns. A basic English/German/French dictionary can be found in Appendix C at the back of this guidebook.

A welcome sight – a sign for a mountain buvette on the Pâturage de la Montagne (Stage 5)

MONEY

Switzerland deals in the Swiss Franc (CHF). Despite Switzerland not being in the European Union (EU) or using the euro, the euro is commonly accepted throughout Switzerland, especially at large hotels. Swiss ATMs offer euros as well as the Swiss Franc in some cantons. Banks usually open Monday to Friday during working hours, alongside having an extensive lunch break. It is advisable to carry cash on you when walking the route, as some buvettes do not have access to Wi-Fi for card payment.

WHAT TO TAKE

If you are staying in dormitory-style lodgings a **sleeping bag liner** is generally required. Silk mummy-shaped ones are the lightest to stow away in your backpack. A **headtorch** with **spare batteries** are essential pieces of kit in the event that you get lost and need to navigate in the dark. In the summer months, sunset takes place between 2000 and 2100 generally, although this does not negate the need to take sufficient emergency lighting. Do try to keep the weight of your backpack below 10–12kg, including a minimum of 2 litres of water to remain hydrated. Other items you will need include:

- **Boots:** comfortable, lightweight, broken-in boots, with ankle support and a good grip on the soles, essential due to the rocky terrain that you will encounter throughout the trail

- **Waterproofs:** breathable waterproof jacket and trousers are essential even in the summer
- **Clothing:** a wicking base layer, fleece mid-layer and an insulated outer
- **Hat and gloves:** highly recommended, even in the summer
- **Sun hat, lipsalve, suncream and sunglasses:** a lot of the high plateaus of the Jura are exposed, with limited cover from the sun
- **Trekking poles:** lightweight telescopic trekking poles are extremely useful to help to redistribute some of the load on the upper body and reduce the impact on the knees.

MAPS

The Swiss have produced very detailed online mapping, considered to be some of the best in the world, that can be downloaded to electronic devices and used offline. Some platforms provide it free of charge, for example Switzerland Mobility, an online free tool to find hikes, bikes, paddles, ski tours and snowshoeing throughout the country. Public rights of way can be discovered, alongside recommended routes.

Swiss paper maps are beautiful, intricately detailed pieces of art. You can purchase waterproof, tear-resistant mapping online, as well as download files, from the Federal Office of Topography, otherwise known as Swiss Topo. As with Harvey's Maps in the UK, the hiking scale is generally considered to be 1:33,000, although 1:50,000 is recommended if you are completing the full trail to minimise the number of maps you need to carry.

If opting for the Swiss Topo 1:50,000 maps, you would need the following sheets to cover the full route:

Waymarkers along the Jura Crest Trail: Bergweg and Wanderweg (Stage 1)

- **Stage 1:** 215T Baden
- **Stage 2:** 214T Liestal (only a small part of this map is used)
- **Stages 2 and 3:** 224T Olten
- **Stages 4 and 5:** 223T Delémont
- **Stage 5:** 233T Solothurn (only a small part of this map is used)
- **Stages 6, 7 and 8:** 232T Vallon de Saint-Imier
- **Stages 8, 9 and 10:** 241T Val de Travers
- **Stages 10, 11 and 12:** 251T La Sarraz
- **Stages 12, 13 and 14:** 260T Saint-Cergue

Alternatively, Kümmerly and Frey cover the Jura Crest Trail at 1:60,000 on sheets 3 (Jura), 4 (Basel), 5 (Aargau), 8 (Neuchâtel), 15 (Lausanne – Vallée de Joux) and a small part of sheet 21 (Geneva). They also cover the first third of the trail at 1:50,000 on sheets 9 (Baselland), 10 (Aargau) and Jura (15).

WAYMARKING AND TRAILS

The Jura Crest Trail (also known as the Jura High Route) is regarded as a Swiss classic. The first official way-marked paths were placed in 1905, and the route has since become one of seven national long-distance paths. Therefore, the route is generally clearly marked. There are some places where the markers are hard to find, sometimes due to fencing being relocated, but these parts are clearly identified in the route descriptions contained in the guide.

A large part of the high alpine pastures and slopes of the Jura have been laid to *bocage* farming, where small sections of farmland have been interspersed with drystone walls and fences; a farming technique more suited to the area, as due to the undulating terrain it is unsuitable for machinery. This leads to a signifi-cant number of footpaths being laid throughout the Jura, and therefore the hiker needs to be vigilant and remain on the Jura Crest Trail and not be dis-tracted by additional paths which may take them off the main route.

The signs and walking routes are maintained by the Swiss Hiking Association. Sometimes yellow diamonds are painted on trees, rocks and fences to identify the hiking route. Remember, all hiking paths in Switzerland are identified by yellow markers so be sure to follow the correct one!

Trail classification

There are two main types of paths found in Switzerland. **Wanderweg** hiking paths are identified with yel-low markers. These paths are gener-ally well maintained and remain at a low altitude for easy hiking for those with a reasonable level of fit-ness. These trails are waymarked by yellow diamond signs with a hiker printed in black, or as flashes of yel-low paint on rocks or identifiable, prominent features such as walls and trees.

Bergweg mountain paths are identified by red and white markers.

These paths generally venture higher in altitude and are more demanding in terms of exposure, difficulty underfoot and steepness. Bergwegs require a safe step, using appropriate walking footwear, alongside the need to orientate yourself and have a good level of fitness.

The route is generally waymarked with yellow signs, some of which are adorned by a large black number 5, with a green square in the background. Only Stage 1 contains a small section of Bergweg, which involves walking along a fairly exposed ridgeline, with steep drops either side.

The grading of terrain, as acknowledged within each stage, can be identified as the following:

Hiking trail (Wanderweg)

Yellow diamonds
Swiss Alpine Club: T1

- Easy conditions
- Recreational walking trail, clearly defined path
- Limited challenging terrain, although sometimes can be moderate to difficult with rocky sections underfoot when wet
- No specialist equipment required
- Signage approximately every 10 minutes.

Mountain trail (Bergweg)

White-red-white rectangles
Swiss Alpine Club: T2 and T3

- Moderate to difficult conditions
- Path can sometimes have exposed ridges or edges with steep drops (slipping, sliding and rockfalls possible)

A traditional Jura inn on the Salhöhepass (Stage 2)

- Difficult sections are secured with fixed ropes or chains to assist movement
- A good level of physical fitness is required.

SAFETY IN THE MOUNTAINS

The majority of walkers will set out and accomplish the Jura Crest Trail with minimal issues. It is well signed and waymarked, and close enough to habitation for you to contact help or relocate yourself. On several stages there are remoter sections, over rocky ridgelines where care must be taken. All who begin the journey must set out fully prepared and able to deal with accidents and emergencies should they arise.

SAFETY IN THE MOUNTAINS

As on any walk, some general points apply:

- Plan your route in advance. Make use of this guidebook, mapping and suitable recommendations as to routes, distances and times.
- Be physically and mentally prepared for the route you intend to take.
- Ensure clothing and equipment is safe and ready to use.
- Plan each day carefully, ensuring you are able to reach your final destination at the end of the day in plenty of time before sunset.
- Take sufficient food and water to last the day, stopping off on route to re-fill where necessary.

- Carry up-to-date mapping and a compass. Do not rely on electronic devices alone, as they may get wet, run out of battery or stop working.
- Keep to designated footpaths and do not take shortcuts.
- Inform somebody of your planned activities, checking-in with them at the end of the day, so that somebody knows your route. In the event of an accident, remain calm, move yourself and the injured person to safety if possible, away from danger. Apply immediate first aid, calling for help if needed. Ensure you and the casualty are warm, then make a note of all the details.

Jura cows (Stage 4)

The main health issues hikers on the Jura Crest Trail face are sunburn, dehydration and blisters. Be sure to wear appropriate sun protection, drink plenty of fluids and treat hot spots as soon as they develop.

The Jura is subject to changeable weather so it is important that you check the weather forecast before leaving: see Appendix B for details of weather forecasting websites. In the high summer, it is recommended that you check during the day as well, as storms generally hit during the afternoon following warm, humid periods. Keep an eye out for a change in the weather as you progress through the day. If a storm is likely, stay away from ridges and high points. If you do get caught in a storm, avoid isolated trees, discard any metallic objects and kneel or squat on your backpack with your head and hands between your knees.

Switzerland does not currently have any major health problems although the last two seasons has seen an increase in the number of ticks, especially in the Jura region. Ensure you use a recommended spray to prevent getting bitten, as well as carrying a tick remover; wear covered shoes and long trousers during the months of April to October, checking regularly throughout the day.

Encountering cows on footpaths is a regular event and may pose some hazards. While attacks are rare, they can occur, especially when the herd contains calves (late spring to early summer). Cows can get aggressive and suddenly charge if they feel you are threatening their calves. Likewise, young calves can be quite inquisitive and playful. Dogs should be on a lead, and keep a wide berth as you pass and make sure the cow has seen you in advance.

Insurance

The cost of an emergency in Switzerland will be high. A European Health Insurance Card (EHIC) grants access to healthcare at a reduced cost, covering state-provided treatment for individuals who have an in-date card: however, it is possible that this may change after Brexit, so check current details. There is no free hospital treatment or rescue, therefore you should take out sufficient insurance prior to beginning your trip, ensuring that it covers you for all activities and includes helicopter rescue.

EMERGENCY NUMBERS

- European emergency number: tel 112
- Police: tel 117
- Ambulance: tel 144
- REGA (mountain rescue): tel 1414

USING THIS GUIDE

The Jura Crest Trail is described heading from the north-east to the south-west and has been broken into 14 stages (summarised in the 'Route summary table'). Each stage is a recommended day's walk, some of which are substantial. Accommodation, amenities and provisions are identified in the route description to assist with planning and help tailor the route to your individual needs. There are also suggested itineraries that offer alternative start and finish points should you wish to only cover part of the trail, or take longer than 14 days, to either go slower and incorporate some sightseeing during your stay.

A map accompanies each stage, although it is not intended to replace paper or digital mapping, but instead should be used in conjunction with larger scale maps for ease of planning and quick reference. A profile also accompanies each stage, to assist with the planning of your daily hikes. Some days begin with quite steep ascents, which you may choose to complete the night before, staying at accommodation recommended at the beginning of the next stage. A kilometre figure is given for each accommodation option indicating the distance each option is from the start of the day's stage.

Statistics and an overview of the day's route is provided at the beginning of each stage, with timings and distances to assist with your planning. They do not take into account water and food stops, or sightseeing along the route. Hikers walk at differing speeds, therefore timings need to be considered. If you find after the first day that you are considerably slower or faster, calculate the next stage

Descending the final stage to Nyon (Stage 14)

Summit of Mont Tendre (Stage 12)

accordingly, to ensure you are planning ahead: an earlier or later start time may be needed.

Transport options are provided for each stage, offering an overview of public transport links to and from the start and end of each stage, alongside opportunities to access accommodation off the main route in order to shorten the length of the stage.

Grading

In addition to the Wanderweg/ Bergweg distinction, within this guide additional information is presented about the trail conditions on each stage. These have been simplified into three grades:

- **Easy:** Shorter stage on easy terrain, with a limited total ascent.

The route predominantly lies on wide, easy to navigate footpaths.

- **Moderate:** Longer stage that may cover more distance and/or include sections of steep, rocky or slippery terrain.

- **Hard:** A strenuous walk where stages may cover more distance, involve a greater ascent and/or include prolonged sections of steep, rocky or slippery terrain. There may be exposed sections requiring good footing and a good head for heights.

THE JURA CREST TRAIL
(EAST TO WEST)

View from the summit of the Belchenflue looking east towards Dielsdorf (Stage 3)

45

STAGE 1
Dielsdorf to Neustalden

Start point	Dielsdorf (428m)
Distance	30km
Total ascent	1120m
Total descent	950m
Grade	Moderate to hard
Time	9hr 30min
Terrain	An exposed ridgeline; the Burghorn path is categorised as Bergweg and is narrow and rocky
High point	Hochwacht (849m)
Accommodation	Jugendherberge Baden (Baden) 12km, Jugendherberge Brugg (Brugg) 25km, Gasthof Bären Bözberg (Neustalden) 31km
Transport options	Trains to Dielsdorf from Rapperswil and Niederweningen (regular, daily), linking with the regional Swiss railway line; buses to Regensberg (hourly); buses from Neustalden to Brugg, Frick and Bözberg (regular, daily)

The first stage of the Jura Crest Trail is arduous, mainly due to its length rather than the terrain. However, it is a pretty stage characterised by towns and villages along the route such as the medieval hilltop settlement of Regensberg, and the lively cities of Baden and Brugg. The route is interspersed with gentle slopes, meandering rivers and lush vineyards and the area has been famous since Roman times for having Switzerland's most mineral-rich springs.

Dielsdorf is a small town providing access to the Jura Crest Trail via the numerous transport options located in the centre of the conurbation. Famed for its horse-racing track, the leading equestrian centre in Switzerland, as well as for having a 400-year-old oak tree with an 11.5m-high trunk in the nearby Schwenkelbergwald forest, Dielsdorf provides ample amenities and accommodation options to begin the Jura Crest Trail.

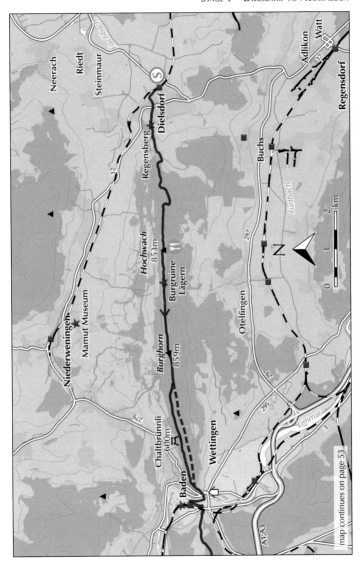

map continues on page 53

47

From the train station at **Dielsdorf**, turn right as you exit where a yellow Wanderweg (German word for trail) post with several yellow hiking signposts can be found. ◄ Take the road west gradually ascending to the main road, walking approximately 100 metres to the yellow hiking path sign identifying the footpath (named Bahnhofweg) right, through a housing estate. Follow the footpath for 250 metres, continuing straight on the path, veering around to the left, cross over onto a cobbled road that goes behind the restaurant and guesthouse Löwen.

This is the official start to the route.

Follow the path along the pavement until you ascend to the main road. Turn right and cross over the pedestrian crossing, heading onto a narrow cobbled lane ascending steeply before continuing up a narrow cobblestoned footpath named Vorderer Breistelweg to garden allotments. Cross over the paved road to continue on a gravel footpath between small isolated orchards, vineyards and allotments. As you near the top of the path, veer right onto Breistelweg passing a small nature reserve as you ascend steeply to the village of **Regensberg**.

Regensberg has a long-standing history as a hilltop fortified settlement. It was founded by Baron Lüthold in 1245, but in the following decades relations between the city of Zurich and the barons soured, as did relations between the barons

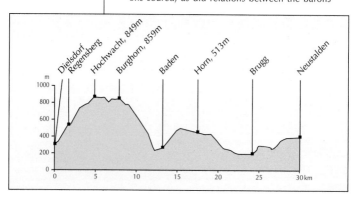

Approaching the medieval village of Regensberg

and the Habsburgs due to conflict over the ownership of lands in the local area. War ensued with the combined Zurich and Habsburg forces victorious and, in 1302, the barons sold Regensberg to the Habsburgs. The appearance of the town belies this shaky start. Today it is a picture-perfect example of Swiss-German architecture, with Schloss Regensberg, the manor house, sitting at its centre.

Enter the town at the east end, passing into the main square of the Oberburg (upper castle) and water well where you have full view of the Rundturn (round tower), the only remnant of original castle. As you near the castle ruins, turn left and pass through the gate between the Oberburg and Unterburg (lower castle), following the cobbled road downhill to the main road. Cross over heading south-west gradually ascending the paved road (Staldernstrasse) for 250 metres, veering right before taking the footpath directly north. The path is narrow and rocky, sweeping left through woodland before joining a

49

gravel road separating the forest on the left and an alpine pasture on the right. At the top of the clearing there is a picnic area and fire pit, before the road narrows slightly into a forest road, gradually ascending. Follow the yellow markers, turning right at the T-junction to join a more defined road up to the **Skyguide Lägern Radar station** and **Restaurant Hochwacht** (853m).

The road narrows into a hiking path with some areas of mountain trail (red/white signs on yellow hiking paths) along the forested ridgeline towards the Burghorn. The trail is partly difficult to access due to steep, narrow and sometimes exposed tops. You need good footwear, a head for heights in a few locations and to be aware of the dangers of slipping or sudden changes in the weather along this ridgeline. ◀ After approximately 500 metres you pass the **Burgruine Lägern**.

> A metal information plaque on a wall at **Burgruine Lägern** details the ruins of a hilltop castle and fortification, used during local feuds of the 13th century. During this time, a small settlement would have existed here, alongside fortifications for potential threats in the area.

Continue along the ridge to the exposed summit of the **Burghorn** (859m) where commanding views can be taken in of the majestic Alps to the south and the rolling Jura to the north. Gradually descend into the woods along the Lägern saddle on a wider footpath until you reach a warning sign informing you of dangerous exposed steep sections ahead. The Jura Crest Trail begins its gradual descent right, down the footpath.

Alternative route along the ridgeline

There is an option here to take the mountain trail ahead, along the ridgeline to Baden, but it is steep and very exposed. At 3km it is shorter than the main route, but the terrain means that it takes a similar amount of time. This route is not too dissimilar to a British grade 1 scramble, whereby the use of hands and feet may be needed due to

The ridgeline is great for trekking in spring and autumn because of the abundance of wildflowers and mostly deciduous woodland.

the knife-edge ridge and level of exposure. This is classed as a red-white mountain trail (Bergweg).

Take the footpath down through the woods then onto a gravel forest road past the picnic and fire pit site at **Chaltbrünnli** (600m). After 3km the forest road reaches a hairpin bend to the right with isolated views over Baden. Take the footpath descending to the left of the bend, to the top of a long set of stairs with views of Baden's historic centre. Descend to the main road, passing the historic museum of **Baden** before continuing down to the underpass that brings you out at the Holzbrücke, a traditional wooden covered bridge that was built in 1809, passing over the River Limmat. ▶

Brugg is 9km from this point with a walking time of two hours.

> **Baden** is a mineral-rich thermal spring town and cultural centre, revived from its industrial past. It was popular in Roman times, when the town was known as 'Aquae Helveticae'. Today, at just 20 minutes from Zurich, it is a popular commuter town.

A covered bridge leading over the river into Baden

Nineteen sulphurous springs bubbling at a temperature of 47°C can be visited along with other sights such as the Villa Langmatt Museum, Lenzburg Castle and the traditional covered bridges over the River Limmat.

Jugendherberge Baden: Swiss Youth Hostel with self-catering facilities, low-cost. Kanalstrasse 7, 5400 Baden, tel +41 56 221 67 36, **www.youthhostel. ch**. To reach the hostel turn left before the bridge, continuing along the river for 400 metres.

Turn right onto Kronegasse, heading north for 300 metres along the River Limmat, before ascending the stairs to join Badstrasse. The route continues south-west passing through Baden's pedestrianised old town before continuing south on cobble-stoned Stadtturmstrasse. Walk through Stadtturm Baden, and iconic clocktower, turning right onto Obere Gasse ascending up to Strasse Niklausstiege, a narrow pathway by house number 35 Obere Gasse. There is a hiking trail signpost at this crossroads, although it is not very clear which route to take. Ascend a long narrow stairway up to Stein Castle (457m), a ruined tower with commanding views over the city and the Burghorn ridgeline back towards Dielsdorf.

Descend the pathway west, meeting the main road (Rütistrasse) towards Allmend. Gradually ascend onto Allmendstrasse then veer left onto Brenntrainstrasse. Turn left gradually climbing the gravel forest road for 1.2km before arriving at **Restaurant Baldegg** (566m), where there is public transport back into Baden. Turn right onto a farm track to join a paved road up to a five-way junction. Cross straight over, taking the footpath into the mixed woodland for 1km to the picnic and fire pit site just north of **Schwabeberg** (549m). Continue on the forest trail for another 2km towards the spot height and viewpoint at **Horn** (513m). ◄

The 180-degree view from Brugg to Kirchdorf is spectacular, taking in the confluence of the Aare, Limmat and Reuss rivers.

From the viewpoint at Horn, **alluvial fan sites** are visible on the riverbank. These have been

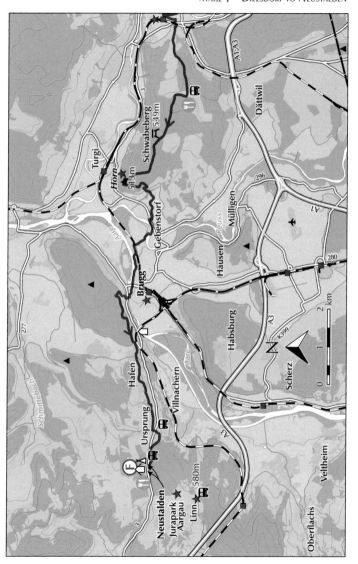

Picnic and fire pit locations as well as swimming areas and diving boards are found on the banks of the River Aare

preserved in a protection park at the 'water castle' (Wasserschloss). This dynamic ecological area sees around one-third of Switzerland's surface runoff pass through this point, therefore preservation from erosion and further damage is of high importance.

Descend the zigzagging footpath through the mixed woodland, passing a Parcoursvita (fitness trail) before reaching a gravel forest road. Turn right, following the path down to the town of Gebenstorf, meeting the paved road. Cross over the road onto a footpath descending steps down across a stream before ascending into a housing estate. Turn right and follow the road until you reach the main road, veering right again, through the main centre of **Gebenstorf** where several restaurants and cafés can be found. Turn left onto Unterriedenstrasse, passing high-rise housing estates before turning right before the bus stop, descending a narrow footpath, down steps through woodland to the main road (Ländstrasse). Using the pedestrian crossing, follow the yellow hiking path signs pointing behind the bus shelter to descend steps to the **River Reuss**.

Follow the riverside footpath, crossing two foot-bridges to re-join the main road, Ländestrasse, to the crossroads. Continue straight, passing under the railway bridge before turning left onto Mühlemattstrasse. Upon reaching the last house, turn right onto a narrow footpath down to the **River Aare**. Continue upstream on a wide footpath, passing under the main road before the footpath detours inland, to join the Falkengasse road passing into the northern end of Brugg. Upon reaching the small pedestrianised area by the side of Hauptstrasse, you have two options. Continue north, passing by the Schwarzer Turm building and over the River Aare, to continue on the Jura Crest Trail. Or to visit the centre of **Brugg** turn left to reach the Rathausplatz and train station. ▶

For reasonably priced accommodation, continue west for 1km along Spiegelgasse, handrailing the River Aare to the historic listed building of the Jugendherberge Brugg.

The town of **Brugg** is situated on the banks of the River Aare. The Romans were the first to bridge the Aareschlucht gorge in 1064, creating a meeting point for important routes throughout this part of Switzerland. Brugg is a stop-off point for amenities, accommodation and onward travel. There are several sights in Brugg, in particular the Vindonissa Museum which houses excavations of the only legionnaire's camp in Switzerland, where you can experience and learn about the Roman's habitation of the town and their day-to-day lives.

Jugendherberge Brugg: Swiss Youth Hostel with self-catering facilities, low-cost. Im Hof 11, 5200 Brugg, tel +41 56 441 10 20, **www.youthhostel.ch**.

Cross over the road at the traffic lights, turning left to a small alleyway that takes you past a castle tower ruin in among houses. ▶ Follow a set of steps, turning right at the top. Follow the road around to the left onto Hansfluhsteig, a cobbled road that climbs steeply into the forest. More steps follow that continue to get progressively more spaced apart until you reach the unpaved

Ursprung is 5km from this point with a walking time of 1hr 10min.

To the south, there is a stunning view straight down the Aare river valley, with the Bernese Oberland Alps in the background.

forest road. Turn immediately left onto a forest path along the top of the ridge overlooking Brugg. The footpath rejoins the forest road to pass a lumberyard, then back onto a footpath that meets a Parcoursvita activity area and car park. Turn onto the paved road, heading west along Parkstrasse to the main road. Turn right then immediately left across the pedestrian crossing onto Gäbistrasse, progressively ascending the road as it goes from paved to gravel to the village of **Hafen**. Follow the yellow signposted route through the village onto an unpaved farm road, Hinterer Hafen. ◀ Join the main road at the village of **Ursprung** where you will find a bus stop and restaurant Vier-Linden.

From the bus stop at Ursprung follow the hiking path signs towards Hauenstein south-west along the farm road Chilemättli. As you reach a fork, take the right-hand path with commanding views dropping away over the River Aare basin and the Alps. Follow the path along the tree line, through a working cattle farm just before reaching the main road. Turn left onto a forest track through

Brugg Old Town

mixed, but mostly deciduous woodland which becomes progressively more coniferous as you continue. The path gradually ascends up to a five-way junction, with a small stream naturally digging a re-entrant to your left. Take the second exit on your left to join an unpaved forest road for 400 metres through a managed forest, mostly coniferous, reaching a crossroads, where woodcarvings left by the foresters can be seen. Turn right, heading north for 400 metres to reach Neustalden, the end point of Stage 1. A basic campsite and guesthouse are located in the small village. ▶

A view of the River Aare, with the Alps in the background, from Ursprung

Another option is to take public transport back to Brugg, if you wish to stay in alternative accommodation.

Gasthof Bären Bözberg: hostel, campsite and restaurant. Book in advance. Neustalden 6, 5225 Bözberg, tel +41 56 441 15 65, gasthof@baeren-boezberg.ch, **www.baeren-boezberg.ch**.

STAGE 2
Neustalden to Hauenstein

Start point	Neustalden (569m)
Distance	29km
Total ascent	1170m
Total descent	1080m
Grade	Moderate
Time	9hr
Terrain	Categorised as a Wanderweg, this stage does have some narrow, rocky paths that can be slippery when wet
High point	Geissflue (963m)
Accommodation	Waldgasthaus Chalet Saalhöhe (Saalhöhe) 17km, Naturfreundehaus Schafmatt (Geissflue) 20.5km, Hotel Froburg (Froburg) 27.5km, Gästezimmer Salzmann (Hauenstein) 29km
Transport options	Buses to Neustalden to Brugg, Frick and Bözberg (regular, daily); buses from Hauenstein to Wisen and Olten (regular, daily)

This stage goes through more remote Jura landscape than the initial stage, passing vineyards, rocky outcrops, forest and meadows. A highlight early on in Aargau Jurapark is the legendary 800-year-old linden tree at Linn. The stage crosses over the Staffeleggpass, one of the lowest cols on the Jura, which is well connected with public transport. It provides an earlier finishing point for this stage should you choose to have a shorter day, or alternatively continue to the next col, Salhöhepass, for another option to reduce the length of this leg. Another col is crossed: Benkerjochpass, which until 1801 was the border the between Austria and Switzerland.

Rejoin the Jura Crest Trail at the crossroads and follow the well-maintained forest track. Continue out of the woods, gradually ascending to the main road, turning left which opens up 360-degree views. As you gradually descend into the village of **Linn**, you enter Jurapark Aargau and

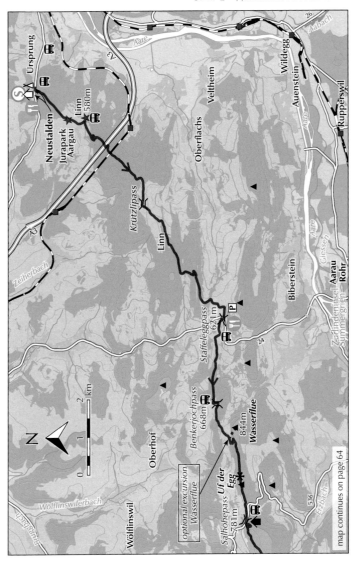

map continues on page 64

59

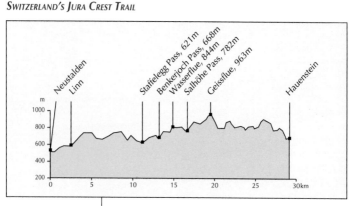

the Lindeplatz (580m) where you pass Switzerland's oldest linden tree isolated among the alpine rolling pastures.

Jurapark Aargau (www.jurapark-aargau.ch) is the largest nature park in the north of Switzerland, covering 244km². Declared a park of national importance in 2012, the majority of the park is found north of the River Aare, on the Jurassic plateau along the Jura Crest Trail. The oldest linden tree (also known as a lime tree) in Switzerland at over 800 years old is found at Linn, within the park. It is over 25m high with a girth of 11 metres, and attracts plenty of visitors. There are benches around the base of the trunk for you to sit and appreciate the magnificent living giant. A bus stop is located next to the tree, providing services to Brugg and other local towns.

Follow the hiking path signs as you continue heading for Staffelegg (12km away, 2hr 30min) on the asphalt road winding its way gently up into the forest. The road ascends onto an unpaved gravel forest track with two back-to-back hairpins before joining a footpath to the left onto a steep, stepped path through predominantly deciduous woodland full of *Allium ursinum*, otherwise known as ramsons or wild garlic. Follow the path around to spot height 722m to access a southeasterly facing viewpoint that drops away rapidly for a stunning view among the trees with a fire pit and benches.

Continue on the footpath to rejoin the forest gravel road after 100 metres, which descends gradually for 1.5km to a junction (665m) with seven paths and several fire pit areas popular with local mountain bikers and hikers. Take the path west (third to the right), out of the forest for 800 metres, along a saddle of alpine grazing land to a small copse, turning left to descend over the **Krützlipass** through pastures still mostly farmed by hand and old sit-on-top tractors, before veering right and gradually ascending into forest again. Continue to follow the hiking path signs gradually ascending up to a ridgeline before descending through the forest for 3.4km. Exit the forest to views of the pepper-pot hills of the Jura and how the range undulates over five main passes. Upon reaching the car park (659m), turn right onto Hauptstrasse to descend via the main road to **Staffeleggpass** (621m). ▸

From here you can catch public transport down off the col to Aarau and Frick, or you can stay and rehydrate in Restaurant Staffelegg.

Looking towards the village of Linn

Cross Staffeleggstrasse to join the footpath through arable pastures and alpine meadows, turning left onto an unpaved farm road up to the Juraparkkäse farmhouse where you can purchase locally produced cheese. Turn left, due west, to gradually ascend to the end of the farm path where it meets a footpath that steeply ascends the edge of the field up steps to meet a farmhouse. Turn left to pass in front of farm buildings before descending into ancient, mature beech woodland. Gradually ascend along a forest road. The path opens up into arable pastures to meet the car park and bus stop at the **Benkerjochpass** (668m). Turn left to gradually ascend to the main car park, fire pit and picnic area. ◀

The route between Staffeleggpass and Benkerjochpass follows the former (pre-1801) border with Austria.

Following the hiking path towards Salhöhe, gradually ascend the unpaved farm road into the nature reserve and deciduous woodland. As you exit into alpine pastures, the Wasserflue ridgeline and summit alongside antenna station appears to the south. Continue descending to the woodland, passing the turn off to the right to Schwefelschür, a family run farm that sells locally produced cheese. After 100 metres, take the footpath steeply ascending (zigzagging) to the spot height 817m. The route turns right here, continuing on to the Salhöhepass.

To visit the Wasserflue
A worthwhile excursion at this point is to ascend the Wasserflue summit (844m), passing the antenna station along the way, via the ridgeline. This is a hiking path (yellow), although sometimes it is difficult underfoot with tree roots and rocky outcrops on the narrow footpath. In places steep drops can be found on either side of the ridgeline, as on a mountain-hiking path (red/white). The extra effort is worth it for the stunning summit viewpoint with 180-degree panoramic vistas from north-east to south-west, overlooking the Jura and the Alps. Return back to spot height 817m to continue on the path.

Follow the top of the ridgeline west on a footpath through well-managed woodland full of wildflowers and a variety of deciduous trees. The path is rocky in some places, with

The view towards the Bernese Oberland from Wasserflue

some views through the trees. At **Uf der Egg** (823m) there are views north over to the summit of Einolte (708m). Descend the steep winding path to join a wider forest path, crossing a paved road, opening up views down the valley towards Wölflinswiller Bach. Continue on a footpath along the tree line, passing a military bunker to **Salhöhepass** (781m). This is a perfect location to shorten the day should you wish, by utilising the public transport at the col to travel south into the larger town of Aarau for various accommodation options, or else continue to Hauenstein (13km and 3hr 40min walking time from this point).

> Waldgasthaus Chalet Saalhöhe: hotel and restaurant. Saalhöhe 156, 4468 Kienberg, tel +41 62 844 10 14, lucek@chalet-saalhoehe.ch, **www.chalet-saalhoehe.ch**.

Pass the Waldgasthaus, continuing northwest on Saalstrasse for 50 metres. Take the first left onto a gravel forest road that gradually ascends, winding its way through a managed mixed woodland before turning left onto a footpath. Continue on the hiking trail following the yellow markers through a series of forest paths and roads for approximately 2.5km, taking in what appears to be an old gun emplacement leftover from bygone

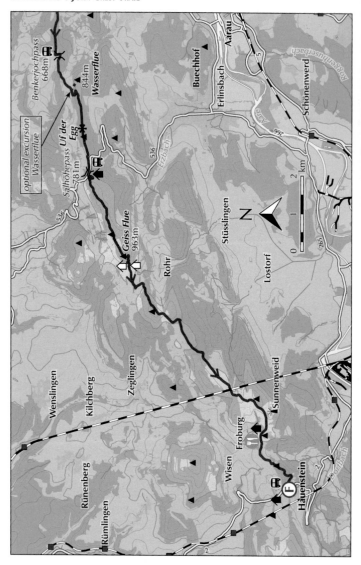

military days. ▶ Here a northwesterly facing viewpoint of 180 degrees over the northern Jura at the summit of the **Geiss Flue** (963m) provides a perfect location for a rest.

Descend the steep, well-maintained footpath through the woods, where it gradually opens up to meet the Berghaus Schafmatt, a beautifully located nature lovers' bunkhouse and restaurant.

> Berghaus Schafmatt: bunkhouse and restaurant (book in advance, low cost). 4494 Oltingen, tel +41 78 803 40 98, info@schafmatt.ch, **www. schafmatt.ch**.

Join the paved road, descending to the main road, where you turn left to gradually ascend, before following the hiking path signs south-west. Pass under the pylon before making a long and gradual ascent of 900 metres through young deciduous wood, mostly formed of beech trees. As you descend out of the forest you pass two picnic and fire pit locations before following the tree line to join an unpaved forest road. Descend this road for 1.5km until reaching a crossroads. Do not continue on the forest road, instead take the easily missed steep narrow footpath (789m) on the bend. Head south-west, contouring around a re-entrant for 300 metres, below a rocky outcrop.

As you pass through a turnstile at the end of the woods, an open footpath is followed south-west for 1km across alpine pastures, before reaching a paved road heading towards a farm building. Pass to the right of the farm, taking the dog-leg re-routed path to miss the farm, before a gradual ascent towards the antenna at **Sunnenweid** where the path gradually becomes a rough gravel farm track. Descend down to the paved road towards **Froburg** taking the farm road to the right beside the bench and picnic area after 100 metres.

> Hotel Froburg: hotel and restaurant. Froburgstrasse 262, 4634 Wisen, tel +41 62 293 29 78, info@restaurant-froburg.ch, **www.restaurant-froburg.ch**.

A demarcation marker informing you of your entry into the canton of Solothurn can be seen.

From a viewpoint looking west towards Hauenstein

Follow the hiking path signs down the farm road to meet the paved road. Follow this over the brow of the hill towards Wisnerhöchi and Hauenstein for 700 metres. The trail leads off the paved road at the tree line on the left-hand side, ascending a footpath up along a ridgeline over spot height 807m, before descending with views over the valley before reaching **Hauenstein**. Re-join the paved road, turning left into the village.

HAUENSTEIN

In days gone by Hauenstein was an important mountain pass, linking 'Augusta Raurica', an old settlement 20km east of Basel, and the 'Mittelland' (the Swiss central plateau) during Roman times, and more recently the city of Olten with Basel. However, a railway tunnel built through the Jura passing underneath Hauenstein in 1858 was the start of the area's demise. Hauenstein is now a quiet mountain town with some amenities, accommodation and transport links, although more options are available in nearby Olten.

Gästezimmer Salzmann: bed and breakfast (phone ahead and book in advance). Oberdorf 2, 4633 Hauenstein, tel +41 62 293 24 55, ly.salzmann@bluewin.ch.

STAGE 3
Hauenstein to Balsthal

Start point	Hauenstein (668m)
Distance	21km
Total ascent	1000m
Total descent	1150m
Grade	Easy to moderate
Time	7hr
Terrain	Generally an easy route, although the path narrows into tracks with exposed rock, in particular when approaching the Belchenflue
High point	Belchenflue (1099m)
Accommodation	Hotel and restaurant Chilchli (Bärenwil) 9km, Genussgaasthaus Tiefmatt (south of Holderbank) 13km, Hotel Balsthal (Balsthal) 21km
Transport options	Buses to Hauenstein from Wisen and Olten (regular, daily); train from Balsthal to Oensingen (twice hourly), which links with the regional train; buses between Balsthal, Oensingen and Ramiswil (regular throughout the day)

The first half of Stage 3 offers an insight into Swiss military history, following a trail of rock paintings and decorations displaying coats of arms, military insignia and leftover World War I and World War II memorabilia. The Belchensüdstrasse along the southern flank of Belchenflue was a main supply route to the World War I fortifications in the area, to prevent German invasion. Soldiers began work in 1914 and the mountain road has remained unchanged since, demonstrating exceptional Swiss engineering and craftsmanship.

Nearing the end of the route, a short climb up through a craggy path brings you out on the Roggenflue plateau, a forested ridgeline filled with locally crafted wooden crosses that opens up a craggy panoramic viewpoint south-west over the Jura. The route passes through the eastern end of Thal Nature Park in Balsthal, an extensive protected nature area that is remote,

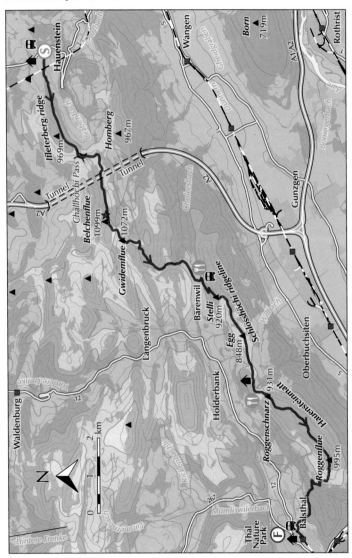

quiet and with fewer tourists. A descent through farmland and forest interspersed with rock crags gently leads to the town of Balsthal and the end of the stage.

From the main road through Hauenstein, turn left and use the pedestrian crossing before heading west along Lantelstrasse towards Kesselberg for 700 metres. Turn left onto a gravel forest road, ascending gradually for 2km under the **Ifleterberg ridge** (969m) to the north, with isolated views across the valley south towards Homberg (967m). From here the road drops off steeply to the south to reveal the limestone craggy summit, as well as the summit of Belchenflue to the south-west. ▶ Descend out of the woods towards a picnic area.

The topography of the Jura at this point presents as a series of undulating pepper-pot hills due to the folded strata, with some sharp, exposed scarp crags.

The extent of **Swiss military preparations** becomes clear here and is far-reaching. You pass through what appears to be a strip of farmed metal girders protruding dangerously out of the lush pastures. These are in fact remnants of past world wars when Switzerland was left to defend its borders against Germany, precariously placed to slow down the movement of enemy troops.

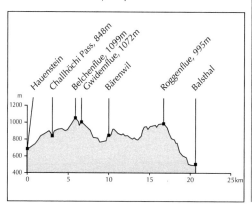

The pass acted as the frontline of defence during World War I and Swiss regiments dug into the rock of the Belchenflue to provide strategic positions to outwit their potential enemy.

The summit is a slight diversion off the Jura Crest Trail, but the 40m of extra climbing is worthwhile.

The view west leaving Hauenstein

Pass through the defensive line, turning left and then right passing a car park before continuing on the gravel road in a southeasterly direction, over the **Challhöchi Pass**. ◀ Follow the historic and gradually ascending gravel road along the south side of the Belchenflue. As you ascend to the summit via this impressively built military road on the steep mountainside known as the Belchensüdstrasse, take note of the military insignia carved and painted into the rock face. Continue on the stepped path from the hairpin bend up to the summit of **Belchenflue** (1099m) for 360-degree views of the area. The pass forms the watershed of the Aare River (south) and the Ergolz (north), which both flow into the Rhine. ◀

Extension to the pass between Ruchen and Belchenflue

A worthwhile extension is the additional 200 metres climb up the gravel road from the hairpin bend, lined with bunkers and fortress doors, to the pass between Ruchen (1123m) and Belchenflue (1099m). If you

View from the summit of the Belchenflue, looking north-west, over the tank grubens

continue north-west down the access road towards Chilchzimmersattel, you can view more tank traps, otherwise known as toblerone trails in Switzerland as well as tank grubens, which are large holes dug into the ground and then later disguised so that invading tanks fall in and are stopped in their tracks in entering the country further.

From the hairpin bend on the gravel road, take the footpath through a turnstile, to descend a series of steps, meandering your way down into an open pasture to join a farm road along the base of **Gwidemflue** (1072m). Bear left onto a forest path ascending to a saddle before descending through alpine pastures to a crossroads. Take the right (narrow and uneven) footpath down to a stream where it opens up into a beautifully carved ravine with overhanging rock sides. ▶ Just before exiting the woods onto a gravel farm road to a picture-postcard Swiss chalet, there is a large picnic area at the confluence of the

The path is muddy and slippery as it forms part of the catchment area for the stream.

Along this road you pass one of over 300 deer farms to be found in Switzerland; venison is eaten throughout the country in similar quantities to other meats.

river. Continue to follow the river, joining an unpaved road through another ravine which divides the cantons of Basel and Solothurn, before opening up to exposed pastures for 800 metres to reach **Bärenwil** (777m). ◀ The village has public transport as well as some basic amenities.

> Restaurant Chilchli: hotel, café and restaurant. Bärenwil 193, 4438 Langenbruck, tel +41 62 390 11 13, Stefan.aegerter@gmx.ch, **www.chilchli.ch**.

SWISS CHALETS

Typical Swiss chalets can be seen throughout the Jura. These traditional wooden building designs characterised by wide projecting, gently sloping gabled roofs and intricately carved wooden balconies are found not just in Switzerland, but throughout the Alps. The Swiss chalet design became famous and originated during the Romantic era of the late 18th century, when noble landowners appreciated and were impressed by the idea of a simple, but homely, outdoor life in the mountains. The design is perfect for alpine conditions, insulating the residence in the winter and remaining cool in the summer, and has remained a strong favourite throughout the country.

As you pass through the village, Restaurant Chilchli and a freshwater fountain are located on your left-hand side, providing hydration and a place of rest. Continue in a south-east direction to the tree line. As you round the bend to the left, turn right onto a gravel forest road and gradually ascend a series of switchbacks before turning left onto a footpath to reach a wide wooden ladder propped up against the steep bank. Use the ladder and continue ascending through mixed woodland until you reach the small saddle of **Stelli** (920m) for views south-east along the **Schlosshöchi ridgeline**. Gently descend around the edge of the pasture with the tree line to your left, walking along the top of a ridge passing **Egg** (848m).

The **Schlosshöchi** is a beautiful rounded ridge carpeted in season with alpine wildflowers. It is divided into small pastures and grazing patches

passed through using a series of turnstiles and gates. There are numerous fire pit and picnic sites established along the ridgeline, providing stunning views of the Alps to the south and the rolling hills of the Jura to the north.

The Jura contains over 950 different flowering plant species

Descend to the paved road, following it along to Genussgasthaus Tiefmatt (809m) a mountain restaurant and hotel with a large terrace with stunning views south down the valley. If you would prefer a quieter location with the comparable views, continue 400 metres southwest along the road where you find a small picnic area with benches, wood oven, fire pit in a spectacular position at the edge of the tree line.

Genussgasthaus Tiefmatt: mountain hotel and restaurant. Tiefmattstrasse 109, 4718 Holderbank, tel +41 62 390 20 60, info@tiefmatt.ch, **www.tiefmatt. ch**.

View of Hällchöpfli, from the Roggenflue

The path is regarded as a hiking (yellow) trail, but for some, it would appear more mountain hiking (red/white).

Continue along the gravel road, gradually turning south to begin the ascent towards the **Hauensteinmatt ridgeline**, an impressive craggy, forested saddle with a viewing platform over Balsthal at the western end. Resume the gentle slope through the grazing pasture to the foot of the Roggenschnarz, where a steep climb begins up steps, some of which are narrow and exposed in places, to summit the ridgeline. ◄

Following the sharp, narrow ascent to the summit of **Roggenschnarz** (931m), the plateau then widens significantly, leaving an expansive footpath winding through the dense forest that sits atop of the ridge. The path continues undulating along forest trails with isolated clearings forming stunning viewpoints of the canton of Solothurn, alongside a substantial number of crucifixes typical of alpine mountain summits.

The alpine tradition of erecting **timber crosses** on the summits of mountains dates as far back as the 13th century. Reasons for doing so ranged from marking alpine pastures or municipal boundaries to early pagan symbols to inhibit bad weather. The crucifix symbol is regarded as overtly religious and generally associated with Catholicism in local areas of the Alps. In recent times some areas of the Alps have seen a rise in summit crosses being vandalised.

The culmination is the viewpoint at the **Roggenflue** (995m), an impressive rocky vantage point with commanding 180-degree views taking in the town of Balsthal, Hällchöpfli and the Jura ridgeline to the south-west and the industrial town of Oensingen to the south.

From the viewpoint, begin the north-westerly descent via a steep, narrow footpath of switchbacks, attempting to stay on the path identified by signs along the way. There are many scree slopes and you can see where mountain bikers and hikers have taken their own route down to the edge of the wood causing significant erosion.

THAL NATURE PARK

The heart of the Thal Nature Park is located in the town of Klus, close to Balsthal, extending across to the Weissenstein summit and north to the Dünnern River. Designated a nature park in 2012, this recently classified area of scientific interest and natural beauty contains most of the local fortress ruins as well as scenic views of high limestone escarpments and deep gorges to explore by foot or on bike. Being located between the cities of Zurich, Berne and Basel, the park is popular with tourists and as such there are plenty of amenities.

As you exit the woods, follow the tree line descending the edge of an alpine meadow, before heading north towards the Hinter Flüeli, a strip of unstable limestone. The path leads you to the end of the crags, descending a track through mixed woodland filled with the smell of wild garlic in spring. ▶ Join the gravel forest road, gently descending for approximately 1km, before Balsthal and the eastern end of Thal Nature Park appears out of the tree line. Continue the gentle descent along the paved road,

The crags rise to around 9m high: the extent and size of the boulders at the bottom bear witness to erosion and movement taking place.

turning left as you enter **Balsthal**, following signs for the Bahnhof and pass under the railway on Postackerstrasse.

BALSTHAL

Balsthal, located on a wide valley following the narrow Klus gorge, has been set in a prominent location in order to defend against enemy invasion since medieval times. Several fortresses surround the historic town, of which many can still be seen today. In particular the 100m-high ruins of the Neu-Falkenstein at Saint-Wolfgang and the local heritage museum situated within the Alt-Falkenstein 12th-century fortress at Klus.

Although Balsthal has only a small population, it has good public transport and is linked to the motorway and regional transport hub just 4km south at Oensingen. The railway line through the Klus gorge was built in 1899 and frequently used to link with the mainline. The line also provides a series of historic train events each year, for example the Chluser Schnägg (Klus Snail steam train).

Hotel Balsthal: hotel and restaurant. Falkensteinerstrasse 1, 4710 Balsthal, tel +41 62 386 88 88, info@hotelbalsthal.ch, **www.hotelbalsthal.ch**.

STAGE 4
Balsthal to Weissenstein

Start point	Balsthal (489m)
Distance	19km
Total ascent	1250m
Total descent	460m
Grade	Easy to moderate
Time	6hr 30min
Terrain	Categorised as a Wanderweg, the trail begins with a moderately steep ascent climbing narrow tracks to Hällchöpfli (1232m), after which alpine pastures are followed
High point	Weissenstein (1279m)
Accommodation	Berggasthof Schwengimatt (south-west of Balsthal) 5.5km, Pension Mittlerer Balmberg (Balmberg) 16km, Hotel and Kurhaus Weissenstein (Weissenstein) 18km
Transport options	Trains to Balsthal from Oensingen (twice hourly), which links with the regional train; buses between Balsthal, Oensingen and Ramiswil (regular throughout the day); cable car/gondola from Weissenstein to Oberdorf to every minute, until 1630

This stage begins with a gradual climb out of town heading for Hällchöpfli, a distance of 5km. After this vantage point, forested paths are followed before opening out onto alpine pastures. Nearing the summit of Weissenstein you pass extraordinary geological features, small viewpoints with ready-made fire pits and a range of stunning wildflowers, shrubs and trees. From the summit panoramic views across the canton of Solothurn can be savoured. The stage then descends through typical rolling Jura terrain across alpine pastures interspersed with Norwegian spruce and wildflowers, with the stage ending with an ascent to the open expanse of the Weissenstein plateau.

From Balsthal Bahnhof turn left onto Postilliongässli, following the road south-east over the level crossing onto

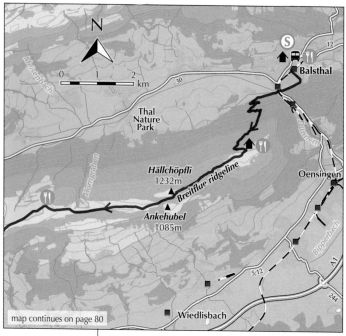

map continues on page 80

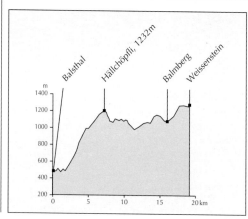

Holderweg which you follow for 400 metres. At the end of the road turn south onto Bisibergweg for 600 metres south-west to reach the main road. Cross the road and bear right then left onto Lebernweg, following the hiking path signs for Weissenstein.

Pass over the level crossing and two streams, along the wood line for 500 metres before entering mixed woodland to begin the long ascent negotiating a series of meandering forest roads and narrow footpaths to the **Berggasthof Schwengimatt** (1000m).

> Berggasthof Schwengimatt: restaurant and hostel. Schwengimatt 50, 4710 Balsthal, tel +41 62 391 11 49, gschneider@bluemail.ch, **www.schwengimatt. ch**. Situated in a commanding plateau position, with seating both indoors and out, in stunning sur- roundings, this is a good place to stay if you are happy to undertake the extra 500m height gain from Balsthal the previous afternoon.

An expansive view over the northern Jura towards Balsthal

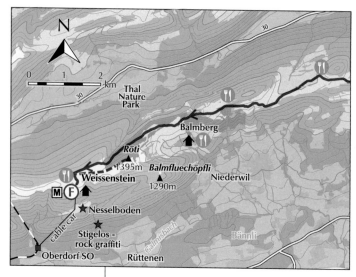

Due to the woodland being embryonic, the floor is scattered with bilberry, wood sorrel, low-lying shrub and a range of wildflowers.

Gradually ascend the alpine pasture south-west on the paved road, veering right onto the gravel farm road past a small copse. As you follow the hiking path along the tree line, views open up to the south-west revealing the towns of Wolfisberg and Oberbipp as well as the Alps, before being enveloped in mixed woodland yet again. The footpath begins to climb the limestone escarpment, passing some exposed steep rock formations, through a young colonising landscape with Norwegian spruces and beech trees. ◀

The gradual ascent nearing the top of the **Breitflue ridge** follows a fence line separating the hiker and an inaccessible paved road weaving its way to an antenna station. The Jura Crest Trail does not pass over the summit, instead just before the footpath descends, take the south-westerly path for 100 metres to eventually reach the top of **Hällchöpfli** (1232m). There is another good viewpoint and picnic area just a minute further on from the turn off to the summit.

A steep and more technical descent zigzags its way down a footpath of steps, maintained paths and steel pegs that protrude in some places and can be slippery when wet. Continue descending through the beech forest to a wider and rockier path then onto a muddy forest road before crossing alpine pastures. Turn right onto a paved road north-west for 200 metres before veering left onto a gravel road for 2.4km. Gradually descend into forest before re-emerging onto alpine pastures, crossing over a saddle with craggy escarpments either side to join a paved road. Follow the road 700 metres, passing **Restaurant Vordere Schmiedenmatt** (also a hostel), before taking the left-hand footpath across gradually ascending open farmland, which progressively becomes a farm road.

Turn left onto the paved road ascending alpine meadows. At the highest point of the road, before it veers right onto a gravel track, a large picnic area and fire pit awaits you with spectacular views south over the Swiss plateau. Continuing west on the farm road you pass **Restaurant**

Mount Röti

There is an
information placard
on the geology of
the area, positioned
at the base of an
overhang with
signposts either
side informing you
of the hazard of
loose rock falling;
exercise caution if
you stop to read it.

Hofbergli (1065m) at the end of the track, with spectacular views behind it of the 1201m-peak Wanneflue and craggy exposed summit of Chamben (1251m) to the north. From the restaurant climb the footpath due-west into the mixed woodland where the track in several places is at risk of rockfall and landslides. ◄

Gradually ascend the footpath through meadows to the gravel road that leads north to the **Restaurant Stierenberg Niederwiler** (1175m). Turn left, following hiking signs descending through forest before arriving at open alpine meadows with views of the exposed summit of **Röti** (1395m) to the south-west. Pass to the north of the small resort of **Balmberg**, where you can find the Seilpark Balmberg (a high-ropes course), a small ski resort, accommodation (Tannenheim Balmberg) and bus stop.

*Restaurant
Stierenberg
Niederwiler*

Pension Mittlerer Balmberg: restaurant and pension offering B&B and half board (500 metres south of the Jura Crest Trail). Mittlerer Balmberg 11, 4524, tel +41 32 637 15 30, **www.mittlererbalmberg.ch**.

WEISSENSTEIN PLATEAU

The Weissenstein plateau offers extensive views across the Swiss Mittelland and the Alps, with the summit peak sitting at 1284m beside the art nouveau style hotel. The Kurhaus offers accommodation, restaurant and access to a free museum charting the history of recreational activities in the area, with information about winter and summer sports, as well as the famous annual motorbike race over the col. You must obtain the key from the hotel reception to access the unmanned museum.

The approach into Weissenstein

The area draws many outdoor enthusiasts offering activities throughout the year such as caving, rock climbing, paragliding, mountain biking, sledging and skiing. The hotel is famous for its health spa, offering milk whey treatments to alleviate illnesses, infirmary and assist with general wellbeing, and has been visited by guests from across Europe for several centuries.Visitors in the 19th century used the route from Weissenstein to Oberdorf as an initial form of exercise and exertion prior to their health recuperation. The steep mountain path from Rüttenen to Nesselboden weaved its way through a labyrinth of impressive rocks at Stigelos. Some rock graffiti from guests, as well as workers who renovated the path, can still be seen on the walls of the stony trail. These days you can also reach Oberdorf via cable car or road.

Kurhaus Museum,
Weissenstein

Turn left to
continue to where
accommodation,
a restaurant and
mountain museum is
located, alongside the
Gondola station that
services Oberdorf.

Pass through the car park (1078m) at Oberbalmberg, crossing over the main road (paved) onto the gravel track. Begin the long gradual ascent through the forest for 2km before emerging on alpine pastures. Towards the top of the ascent, rock falls and landslips are common on one section, especially following periods of heavy rain. Continue in a south-west direction along a wide gravel footpath, contouring along the base of the Weissenstein. The route finishes at the crossroads (1261m) between the footpath and the col road providing vehicular access between Oberdorf and Welschenrohr. ◄

Hotel and Kurhaus Weissenstein: hotel, restaurant and mountaineering museum. 4515, Weissenstein, Oberdorf, tel +41 32 530 17 17, **www.huettenzauber.ch.**

STAGE 5

Weissenstein to Frinvillier

Start point	Weissenstein (1279m)
Distance	24km
Total ascent	800m
Total descent	1550m
Grade	Easy
Time	7hr 45min
Terrain	Wide, clear hiking trails through pastures, steep descent into Frinvillier which can sometimes be challenging underfoot
High point	Obergrenchenberg (1347m)
Accommodation	Berggasthof Untergrenchenberg (north of Grenchenberg) 11.5km, Restaurant Stierenberg (north of Grenchenberg) 13km, Swiss Hostel Lago Lodge (Biel/Bienne) 5.5km, Hôtel La Truite (Pery) 2.5km
Transport options	Cable car/gondola from Oberdorf to Weissenstein every minute, until 1630; bus from Frinvillier to Biel/Bienne (six times daily); train from Frinvillier to Biel/Bienne (hourly)

An informative Planetenweg (planet path) has been set up for the first section of the walk, which has information on the planets as well as the wildflowers that adorn the nearby slopes. As the route progresses south-west, it rises and falls through remote alpine meadows, up forested ridgelines to small summits and along the top of craggy scarp slopes, before reaching gently rolling terrain. Towards the end of the route, the pastures open up to small farming communities and country chalets for the locals along the Pâturage de la Montagne, before the route descends into Frinvillier.

Leaving the car park (1261m) at **Weissenstein**, follow the gravel road south-west, through the Plantenweg, alpine meadows and pastures until the road reaches within 200 metres of the **Gasthof Hinter Weissenstein** (1226m). The

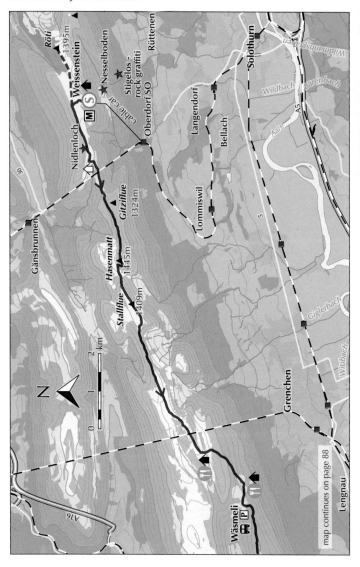

map continues on page 88

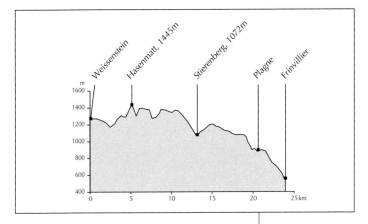

buvette is open from 0800 daily for food and beverages and is less commercialised than the Kurhaus.

> The **Nidlenloch cave system** (www.nidlenloch.ch), just north of the Gasthof Hinter Weissenstein, was first discovered in 1828 and since then has become one of the most famous caves in the canton of Solothurn. With over 6000 potholers visiting each year, the passages follow the dip of the Jura bedding planes for 7.5km in length and to a depth of 418m. The caves have easy access and the first part has a rigged system, although it is highly recommended that you seek the services of an experienced guide should you wish to descend.

Turn left, continuing on the gravel road passing through meadows and alpine pastures for 1km, before entering mixed woodland where the route slowly, then steeply, ascends onto a rocky ridgeline. **Hasenmatt** (1445m) is the highest summit in the canton of Solothurn, affording panoramic views from north-east to south-west across the plain to the Alps beyond.

Descend the path and head north for 150 metres before turning west down to a gravel farm road. Follow

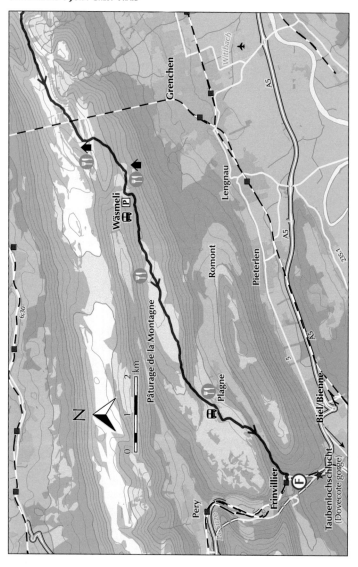

*Berggasthof
Untergrenchenberg*

the track and pass over a saddle before ascending again to reach **Stallflue** (1409m), a 1.5km-long table top plateau of alpine pastures. The route follows an occasionally rocky forest path for 1km, following the top of an escarpment, offering views of the Bettlachstock (1298m) to the south.

For the next 1km you gradually descend on open grassland before reaching the Obergrenchenberg road. Continue south-west to reach **Berggasthof Untergrenchenberg** (1299m) which offers accommodation and food, and regular buses to Grenchen (which has supermarkets and other amenities and transport links to Biel/Bienne) leave from here too. ▶

From here, the hike to Frinvillier takes 3hr 30min.

Berggasthof Untergrenchenberg: B&B and restaurant. Untergrenchenberg 2540, Grenchen, tel +41 32 652 16 43, info@untergrenchenberg.ch, **www.untergrenchenberg.ch**.

Follow the forest path, descending the track which passes the tarmac road three times before turning right, off the path, onto the road nearing the **Restaurant Stierenberg** (1072m).

Restaurant Stierenberg: restaurant and hotel. Grenchenberg 2540 Grenchen, tel +41 32 652 16 44, **www.grenchenberge.ch/grenchenberge/ stierenberg**. The restaurant has panoramic views from the terrace, and traditional menu consisting of a local drink of apple juice with water and sugar.

Continue ascending up the road, passing wild raspberries, until you reach the first gravel road on the left. The signposting can be somewhat confusing due to a conglomeration of paths joining at the same junction and veering off. Turn left on the gravel forestry road before reaching the car park (1102m) at **Wäsmeli**.

The signpost is easy to miss.

Follow the road into the mixed woodland for 400 metres before turning right onto a rocky track. ◄ The track gently ascends through the woods for approximately 1km, onto typical Jura terrain of open rolling grazing pastures. Head west along the gravel road, passing **Restaurant Romontberg** (1120m), a small buvette popular with the many local chalet owners scattered throughout the Pâturage de la Montagne.

Descending steeply down a forest path, you arrive at **Plagne**, a small village with a post office and restaurant, alongside bus links to Biel/Bienne and Romont (number 71). Pass through the village, turning right onto the main street, then immediately left onto Chemin des Oeuchettes. Follow the road to the end, passing through a farm gate onto a gravel farm road heading south for 200 metres. Turn left to follow a track descending gently through pastures, then steeply through mixed woodland to the main road.

The bus stop is located here, for transport into Biel/ Bienne to access amenities.

Turn right onto a narrow rocky footpath to continue descending for 800 metres through woodland before rejoining the main road, the Route Principale providing a gentle road-friendly route into **Frinvillier**. ◄ For the centre of town, cross over the road, descending a grass verge, under the main highway to the train station.

FRINVILLIER

The small village of Frinvillier (516m) lies at the northerly end of a 150m-deep gorge: Taubenlochschlucht (Dovecote gorge). The 3km-long, well-maintained hiking trail follows the centuries-old eroded path of the River Suze (translated as Schüss) past whirlpools, overhangs and other geological formations through the folded Jura. The gorge walk can be accessed via the Leubingen/Evilard cableway in Biel, finishing in Frinvillier.

There is limited accommodation in Frinvillier, although Biel/Bienne, with accommodation aplenty alongside amenities, food provision and onward regional travel, is within 15 minutes of the village by train or bus. Also, 3km north and a six-minute train journey away is the small village of Pery offering hotel accommodation and restaurants.

Swiss Hostel Lago Lodge: Swiss Youth Hostel. Uferweg 5, 2560 Nidau, tel +41 32 331 37 32, **www.lagolodge.ch**. Despite being in Biel/Bienne, it is just 15min by train followed by a short walk. The hostel is well worth the travel time: low cost, clean rooms, great atmosphere and beer brewed on-site.

Hôtel La Truite: hotel and restaurant. Rue de la Reuchenette 3, Pery 2603, tel +41 32 485 14 10, **www.hotellatruite.ch**. In Pery.

STAGE 6

Frinvillier to Chasseral

Start point	Frinvillier (532m)
Distance	18km
Total ascent	1300m
Total descent	310m
Grade	Moderate to hard
Time	6hr 30min
Terrain	Steep, narrow rocky paths, and an ascending narrow ridgeline to Chasseral, some exposed parts
High point	Chasseral (1606m)
Accommodation	Cabane du Jura (Orvin) 7km, Bison Ranch (les Colisses) 14km, Hôtel Chasseral (Chasseral) 18km, Métairie de Dombresson (south-west of Chasseral) 20km
Transport options	Bus to Frinvillier from Biel/Bienne (six times daily); train to Frinvillier from Biel/Bienne (hourly); bus from Chasseral to Saint-Imier (three times daily); bus from Chasseral to La Neuveville (twice daily)

This is a fairly remote stretch of the route with limited buvettes along the way and, thus, it is not at all touristy. It is classed as *wanderweg*, although a large portion of the trail covers tracks that are sometimes through rocky outcrops, ascending a long ridgeline. The beginning of the stage is physically challenging. The 500m steep ascent of the first 3.5km up to Les Coperies follows a forest path through trees with sometimes exposed narrow edges. The final destination, the summit of Chasseral, involves another long ascent, but the extensive panoramic view is a suitable reward.

From the train station at **Frinvillier** head west along Route Principale, passing over the bridge that crosses the River La Suze, which goes on through the Frinvillier gorge to feed the River Schüss. Immediately at the end of the bridge, take the footpath right, ascending a steep weaving path on rocky terrain through the forest for 2km. The trail

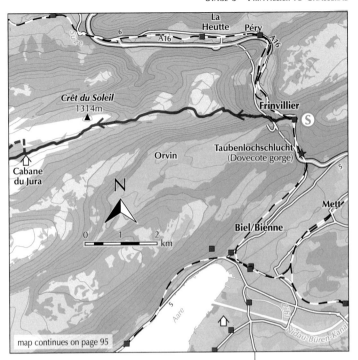

map continues on page 95

elevates above the village and highway, ascending 480m in height, offering occasional panoramas within the forest to give snapshots of what is to come later on the route. Occasionally there are helpful steps cut into the rock, as well as fixed equipment at spot height 858m where a 5m-length chain offers support over an exposed, steep ridge that can be slippery when wet.

Turn right onto a gravel farm road and continue ascending through open pastures passing Les Coperies (1130m), a farm building on the right before a welcome descent through forest. The route again begins a gentle ascent for 1km, passing a farm, La Ragie (1165m), before turning right off the road at a hairpin bend to continue onto a track through open pastures. Follow for a further

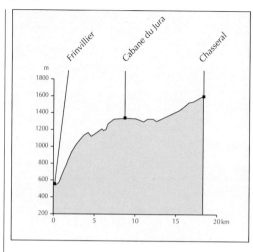

Small chained section assisting a steep ascent, west of Frinvillier

1.5km, ascending to a height of 1338m on the ridgeline, marking the end of an 800m height gain over 6km. The trail gently rolls south-west along the ridge on footpaths

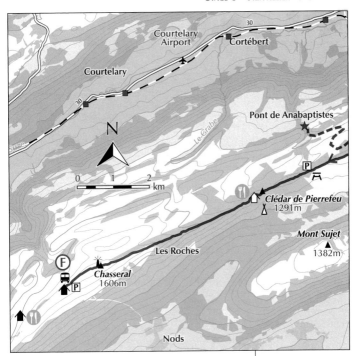

through open pastures with views of the Emmental and the Alpine foothills north-east through south-west. Continue along the ridgeline to **Cabane du Jura**, a CAS mountain hut, at spot height 1322m.

> Cabane du Jura: hut available to both members and non-members (book in advance). 2534 Orvin, www.sac-biel.ch.

To visit the Pont des Anabaptistes
There is an optional detour at this point to see the Anabaptists' Bridge. Turn right, off the Jura Crest Trail, heading north towards Mét de Diesse, a seasonal buvette, 500 metres north of the footpath junction. From here,

Ascending the combe from La Ragie

follow the footpath for 600 metres south-west to meet a tarmac road heading north-west. Follow this for 2km. The road cuts through a deep ravine where the Pont des Anabaptistes can be located.

> The **Pont des Anabaptistes**, a modern architectural design, passes over a small gorge that marked the path and secret meeting spot of the discreet religious group, believed to date back to the 17th century. The Anabaptists took refuge in the Jura to avoid persecution 400 years ago from Catholics and Protestants who attempted to curb the growth of the religious group. Rock carvings that have never been deciphered and remain a mystery can be seen near here.

Return to the Jura Crest Trail the same way you approached.

Continue along the route from Cabane du Jura for a further 1.5km, at which point you begin to descend down into a small picnic area (1288m), popular with the locals due to the tarmac access road from Orvin, which continues to northern villages over the Jura ridge. ◄

The area is interspersed with buvettes and private dwellings.

From the small car park, continue in a south-westerly direction, gently ascending a path through open pastures for approximately 1km, to where a footpath crosses over the trail at **Clédar de Pierrefeu** (1291m). (Take the footpath south-east from here for Bison Ranch, a themed campsite offering accommodation in Wild West tipis, cabins and tents.)

> Bison Ranch: camping (book in advance). Les Colisses 101, 2534 Les Pres d'Orvin, tel +41 32 322 00 24, Christian@bisonbranch.ch, **www. bisonranch.ch**. To reach the site, walk down the footpath until you reach the road, turn right and walk west for 600 metres.

From Clédar de Pierrefeu (1291m), continue 500 metres to **Buvette Les Colisses du Haut** (1338m) situated at the top of a gravel forest road serving a range of drinks. Basic but a perfect fuel stop before the final section of the route: a 6km-long, 320m climb to Chasseral following the ridgeline up to the antenna.

From the buvette, continue in a south-westerly direction, gently ascending through an alpine pasture that opens up out of the tree line to enable panoramic views. The route resumes climbing along the ridgeline for 3km, alternating between wider grass strip pastures and narrow woodland footpaths until it begins to contour gently to a small spot height (1529m). A short descent along

Buvette Les Colisses du Haut

SWITZERLAND'S JURA CREST TRAIL

CHASSERAL NATURE PARK

Chasseral Nature Park extends over 400km², incorporating one of the Jura's highest summits, Chasseral (1606m). More than 500 species of wildflowers and over 20 different types of orchids exist among well-maintained farming pastures and forests. The area has been farmed since the Middle Ages when deforestation took place on a large scale in order to open up grazing land for livestock. A haven for wildlife, the park is rich in chamois, grouse, marmots and pellegrine falcons as well as rarer species such as the woodlark. Throughout the Chasseral plateau, information boards identify and detail different species, as well as giving advice regarding using the park.

The plateau can be explored on foot, bike or horse, with numerous paths dissecting the landscape. The area dominates the Swiss Mittelland, providing panoramic views across the plains of Switzerland and Lac de Neuchâtel to the Alps, as well as extending north over the Franches Montagnes towards the Vosges and Black Forest. Chasseral separates the French- and German-speaking part of the Jura, as well as dividing rural and industrial landscapes. This is an area rich in biodiversity and the park itself is an exercise in conservation. In contrast, the industrialised 120m-high antenna that sits atop of the summit provides telecommunications throughout the region.

the crest leads you above the rocky crag **Les Roches** see below on the southern flank. Be sure to stay on the way-marked track; wandering far from the southern side of the path leads to steep cliffs. Continue following the footpath to the summit of **Chasseral** (1606m), the highest point of the section, as you pass through Chasseral Nature Park.

From the summit, after 1km along the tarmac road and footpath you reach **Hôtel Chasseral** (1548m), which has rooms and refreshments, and there is also a traditional 'sleeping on straw' option, 1.5km west located early on in Stage 7.

Hôtel Chasseral: bar, restaurant and hotel. Route de Chasseral 124, 2518 Nods, tel +41 32 751 24 51, **www.chasseral-hotel.ch** (open year round).

Métairie de Dombresson: sleeping barn. 2057 Villiers, Chasseral, tel +41 32 751 20 10.

STAGE 7
Chasseral to Vue des Alpes

Start point	Hôtel Chasseral (1548m)
Distance	19km
Total ascent	680m
Total descent	950m
Grade	Easy
Time	5hr 45min
Terrain	Mainly wide, easy to navigate paths through rolling terrain
High point	Mont d'Amin (1417m)
Accommodation	Vire de Vie (south of Le Pâquier) 8km, Chalet du Mont d'Amin (east of Vue des Alpes) 16km, Hôtel de la Vue-des-Alpes (Vue des Alpes) 19km
Transport options	Bus to Chasseral from Saint-Imier (three times daily); bus to Chasseral from La Neuveville (twice daily); buses from Vue des Alpes to Chaux-de-Fonds (three times daily)

This stage offers a pleasant day of hiking through rolling farmland and forested areas interspersed with hiking and mountain biking trails. The route sweeps down between the wooded Val de Ruz and Saint Imier valleys to the winter sports resort and industrious village of Le Pâquier, famed for its farriers and horsemen. It passes through the Montagnes de Chézard, a *bocage* landscape dissected with footpaths dating back to the 18th century, before following the ridgeline along Mont d'Amin. The stage ends at the col, Vue des Alpes.

Leaving **Hôtel Chasseral**, rejoin the footpath heading north-east towards the Chasseral antenna for 100 metres to a large alpine cross (1552m) on the ridge of the escarpment, revealing the onward journey south-west through pastures interspersed with Norwegian spruces. Descend the steep footpath south-west for 600 metres crossing the Col du Chasseral road twice. On reaching it a second

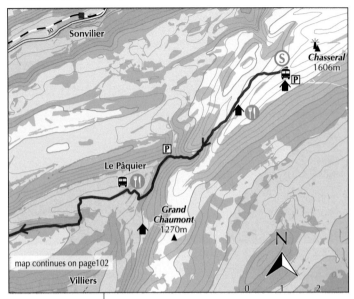

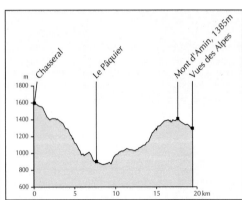

time, ensure you stay to the left-hand side of the road for 100 metres, turning left, onto the unmarked, paved road south-west towards **Métaire de Dombresson**.

The buvette and *métairie*, **Tarte à La Crème** (Métaire de Dombresson), is popular with the locals for its regional dairy products and opportunity to 'sleep on straw' in the summer months, a traditional camping method in Switzerland. Located throughout the Chasseral Nature Park, *métairies* are alpine taverns that produce local cheese, dairy items and meat for you to sample. They are normally located in a buvette, a local farm café or restaurant, serving specialities of the region.

Contour around the grazing pasture, being careful to stay on the path and not to take a trail made by the local herd, before crossing over a prominent drystone wall. Veer right, descending into the wooded Combe Biosse valley to the meet the road, Route des Fontaines, where there is a **car park**. The descent takes you along a path almost like a Roman road of rounded stone, which goes through deciduous woodland of beech, sycamore and birch, making it treacherous when wet.

View west from Chasseral, towards Vue des Alpes

101

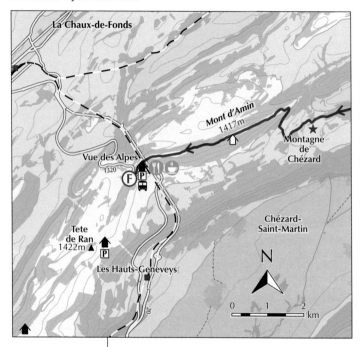

Continue on the footpath through the Forêt d'Aigremont, towards **Le Pâquier**, a village famed for being the hometown of famous World Cup alpine skier Didier Cuche, as well as for its farriers. Do not rely on the water trough in the village, which is commonly empty, but there is a restaurant located north-east on the main road where you can rehydrate. The village has a bus service, but limited accommodation with an airbnb just off route.

Vire de Vie: airbnb apartment. Clémesin 17, 2057 Villiers (1.7km south of Le Pâquier), tel +41 32 853 47 84. Sleeps up to 4 people.

▶ Head west out of the village gradually ascending along the paved road before turning left onto footpaths through grazing land to a ridgeline. Evidence of forestry can be found; be sure to keep an eye out for the yellow footpath markings on trees as you navigate the trail. Due to the number of footpaths in the area, the **Montagne de Chézard** can be a little hard to navigate.

From this point Vue des Alpes is 3hr 10min away.

BOCAGE FARMING

This preserved yet remote area of ancient cultural setting lays claim to a *bocage*-style landscape. It is an area where intensive farming is impossible due to the topography, and so remains as it has been for a number centuries. A map dating around the year 1840 can be compared to identify a limited amount of change in the 175 years since it was produced. In France *bocage* farming is where numerous small plots of agricultural land are interspersed by small drystone walls and hedgerows to form a micro-intensive farming landscape. Traditional farming methods have remained whereby north-south walls have 20-metre-wide gaps to allow for cattle driving and rotation, to ensure the biosphere is utilised to its maximum.

Upon reaching a paved access road, you have the opportunity to turn left and head south to the small watch-making village of Chézard-Saint-Martin. The Jura Crest Trail does not visit the village. Instead the route continues in a south-west direction, before heading north, onto a high ridgeline, **Mont d'Amin**, a typical Jura crest with rocky outcrops where a range of alpine flowers grow throughout the year. From the highest point (1417m), there are commanding views of the surrounding area, as well as the Chasseral summit behind and Lac de Neuchâtel ahead. Some 150m below the summit on the southern wide is **Chalet du Mont d'Amin**.

Chalet du Mont d'Amin: basic CAS hut (must be booked in advance). 2054 Chézard-Saint-Martin, tel +41 32 853 24 26, labovienne@gmail.com, **www.cas-chauxdefonds.ch**.

An informative Nature Park sign giving information about the local area

103

Approaching the village of Le Pâquier

Continue on the trail west-south-west for 1km before joining and ascending a paved road for 300 metres before turning left onto a footpath passing through woodland for 200 metres. The last 2km to the col traverses along the ridgeline, past several holiday chalets, before descending into the col at **Vue des Alpes**.

VUE DES ALPES

The high mountain pass of Vue des Alpes links the lakeside conurbation of Neuchâtel with the watch-making metropolis of La Chaux-de-Fonds. As is common in Switzerland, a tunnel through the Jura provides a high-speed road link which limits the amount of traffic over the col. Public transport is only available (via a train or bus) from the north side of the Jura, where plentiful amenities and accommodation options can be found in La Chaux-de-Fonds. The col provides a range of summer and winter outdoor adventure activities such as mountain biking, hiking, paragliding, snowshoeing, Nordic and alpine skiing, making it a popular destination throughout the year. There are small cafés and restaurants and Hôtel de la Vue des Alpes provides a range of accommodation, in addition to a restaurant, evening entertainment and children's play area.

Hôtel de la Vue-des-Alpes: bar, restaurant, hotel. Vue des Alpes, 2052 Fontaines, tel +41 32 854 20 20, **www.vue-des-alpes.ch**. Open year round.

STAGE 8
Vue des Alpes to Noiraigue

Start point	Vue des Alpes (1283m)
Distance	22km
Total ascent	760m
Total descent	1300m
Grade	Easy to moderate
Time	6hr 45min
Terrain	Some challenging conditions from the Tablettes to Noiraigue where the path is sometimes narrow, rocky and exposed
High point	Mont Racine (1439m)
Accommodation	CAS Fiottet (south-west of Mont Racine) 8.5km, Hôtel de la Tourne (Col de la Tourne) 13km
Transport options	Buses to Vue des Alpes from Chaux-de-Fonds (three times daily), connecting in Le Reymond; trains from Noiraigue to Neuchâtel (hourly); trains from Noiraigue to Buttes (twice an hour)

This stage follows a panoramic high mountain massif, filled with geological beauty. Along the route, Tête de Ran (1422m), Mont Racine (1439m) and the Tablettes (1290m) are summited, before following the high ridgeline and rocky outcrop along the Forêt de Fretereules to reveal the Noirague valley, deep below.

The trail passes through some of the most scenic landscape the Jura has to offer, and also an outdoor mecca for many adventure sport enthusiasts. Nordic and alpine ski runs can be seen along the route, alongside paragliding launch areas, mountain bike tracks and extensive hiking trails, offering the visitor many options should they wish to extend their stay.

From Hôtel de la Vue-des-Alpes, cross over the road, through the car park, following the footpath beside the toboggan run to the top of the ridgeline. A gravel farm

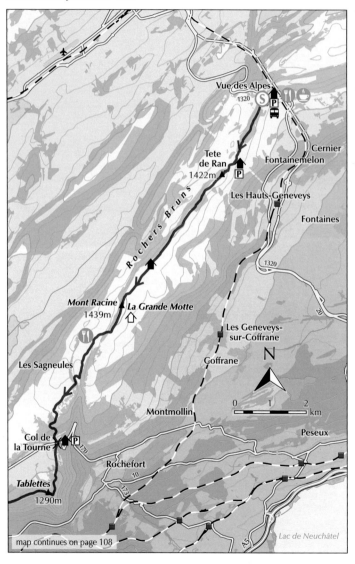

Vue des Alpes
1320
S P

Cernier

Tete
de Ran
1422m
P

Fontainemelon

Les Hauts-Geneveys

Fontaines

R o c h e r s   B r u n s

1320

Mont Racine
1439m

La Grande Motte

Les Geneveys-
sur-Coffrane

Coffrane

N

Les Sagneules

0   1   2
km

Montmollin

Peseux

Col de
la Tourne
P
170

Rochefort

10

Tablettes

1290m

A5

Lac de Neuchâtel

map continues on page 108

106

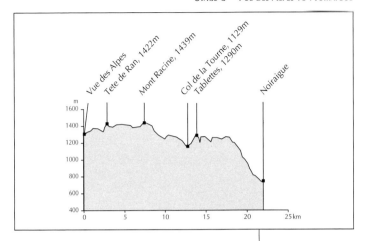

road passes several holiday dwellings and the top of the ski tow, before entering a wooded ridge along a track for 1km. Exit the ridge onto alpine pastures scattered with more holiday dwellings, descending the partially paved

View from above Vue des Alpes, towards the Tablettes

107

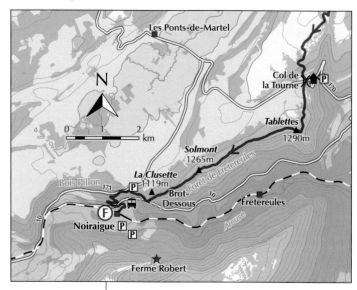

The summit is littered
with evidence of
winter snow sports
and outbuildings
for the servicing of
the uplifts, some of
which are redundant
year round.

road to the Tête de Ran ski school and hotel. Cross over the road, to join a path steeply ascending the numerous switchbacks up to the summit of **Tête de Ran** (1422m). ◄

Continue along the ridgeline, descending slightly, as you pass along the 3.5km edge of **Rochers Bruns**, a craggy escarpment north-west. The gently rolling alpine pastures of the scarp slope south-east reveal a conservation and military area clearly marked by information boards and waymarkers. The military train in the Mont Racine area regularly so avoid straying from the marked path.

Continue descending, past the seasonal buvette **Loge des Pradières-Dessus** (check www.mont-racine.ch if you wish to stop here, as its opening hours are infrequent). After 200 metres cross the road heading south-west, to reveal the extensive military shooting ranges to the south.

Begin the steep ascent up to Mont Racine. As you near the top, it becomes very rocky with exposed limestone making it difficult to follow the exact path. The summit of **Mont Racine** (1439m) rewards with panoramic views. ▸

Gently descend 500 metres from the summit, passing the turnoff left to the CAS mountain hut at **La Grande Motte** (1421m). The hut is 200 metres south-east of the track, just past the intersecting footpath.

CAS Fiottet: Sommartel Section mountain hut. Basic, book in advance, access is only on foot. **www.cas-sommartel.ch**.

Continue another 500 metres, negotiating intermittent rocks, before squeezing through a small gap in the drystone wall; a Swiss preventative measure to stop grazing cattle from escaping. Steeply descend a track through the wooded ridgeline, to buvette **La Grande Sagneule** (1307m), a welcome break and very popular with locals. ▸

The Mont-Racine Trail (a 20km circular cross-country ski track) in winter is regarded as the Jura Himalaya for its high expansive, exposed plateau and bitter winds.

The buvette has an extensive menu with locally sourced food and an open kitchen with traditional log burning stoves throughout.

La Grande Sagneule

Follow the paved road south-west, 200 metres past **Les Sagneules** (1232m), before turning right onto a poorly marked footpath across a marsh area. Be sure to stay on the path as there is a small bridge to help get across the stream. Ascend the footpath to a narrow ledge around a rocky outcrop before entering expansive alpine pastures. After 500 metres join the paved road, continuing south-west, passing Petit Coeurie (1263m), a farm building dug into the surrounding farmland. Descend a further 1km through woodland to the road to the **Col de la Tourne**, to access public transport, a hotel and restaurant.

Hôtel de la Tourne: restaurant and hotel. La Tourne, 2019 Rochefort, tel +41 32 855 11 50, resto. latourne@gmail.com.

Cross over the road, passing through the car park and joining the footpath for a 1.5km gentle ascent to the Tablettes. Along the route south, several disused military bunkers can be seen, before you reach the open meadow below the summit. Be sure to approach the fence line marking the top of the precipice, as the viewpoint can be hard to find, but once at the summit of the **Tablettes** (1290m) the panoramic view across Lac Neuchâtel and the Fribourg mountains can be enjoyed.

The route gently undulates along a rocky footpath on the forested ridge of Forêt de Fretereules for over 5km to the prominent peak, La Clusette. Along the trail the footpath can be narrow in places, with some exposed sections with steep drops, in particular 2.5km along the ridge as you near the summit of Solmont (1265m). Here the path undulates, weaving between rock crags. ◄ Upon reaching the viewpoint and prominent telecommunications antenna at **La Clusette** (1119m), spectacular views of Creux du Van, a geological feature across the valley, west of Noiraigue, can be savoured.

Locals who frequent the area have built fire pits along the route, providing plentiful rest stops.

After La Clusette, the route can be difficult to follow as the via ferrata climbing wall obscures the view ahead

The view from the ridgeline of the Forêt de Fretereules looking down towards the Noiraigue valley

and there are many paths due to tourism, outdoor activities and the workers needing access to the telecommunications antenna at the spot height. Ensure you contour north-west to a defined forested track before beginning to descend. From La Clusette follow the path for 800 metres to reach the start of the via ferrata. Turn left before meeting the small car park and main road to begin the descent to Noiraigue. The path through the **Bois Pillion** is steep and sometimes rocky in places at the beginning, although gradually reduces in gradient as you meet with the forest track.

Cross over the main road (Route 10) immediately to prevent being on a blind corner, before turning left to join Rue Perrin south-west for 200 metres to reach the centre of **Noiraigue** and its amenities.

NOIRAIGUE

Noiraigue is in the perfect location for being a centre of hiking and other outdoor activities. It sits at the eastern end of the Val de Travers on the River L'Areuse, and lies just off the main road with a mainline train station that links Neuchâtel in Switzerland with Pontarlier in France, providing ample public transportation within the canton of Neuchâtel's largest conservation area. The name Noiraigue was derived from Latin in AD998, meaning 'black water' due to the marshland drainage which gives the local waters a black tinge. The impressive river flows from the valley, through the village before descending into the Gorges de L'Areuse. From the village you can take a hiking trail to see the torrents of water flow south-east to the town of Boudry. There are amenities available including a train station, several chocolatiers and a post office.

Hôtel Grill Restaurant (4km off-route): restaurant and hotel. Crêt de l'Anneau 1, 2015 Travers, tel +41 32 863 11 11. There is no accommodation available in Noiraigue after the closure of L'Auberge de Noiraigue. For other nearby options see **www.neuchateltourisme.ch**.

The via ferrata at Noiraigue: the route doesn't go this way!

STAGE 9

Noiraigue to Sainte-Croix

Start point	Noiraigue (733m)
Distance	32km
Total ascent	1700m
Total descent	1400m
Grade	Moderate to hard
Time	10hr 30min
Terrain	A longer stage with a considerable ascent along an exposed path to the top of the Creux du Van. After this point the path is wide and easily navigated through rolling terrain
High point	Le Chasseron (1607m)
Accommodation	Ferme Restaurant le Soliat (near summit of Le Soliat) 5.5km, Camping Les Cluds (Les Cluds) 25km, Hôtel du Chasseron (summit of Chasseron) 25.5km, Chambres d'hôtes Grangette Bellevue (Sainte-Croix) 33km
Transport options	Trains to Noiraigue from Neuchâtel (hourly); trains to Noiraigue from Buttes (twice an hour); buses from Sainte-Croix to Buttes (three times daily); train from Sainte-Croix to Yverdon-les-Bains (hourly)

This stage is pleasantly long and one of the most picturesque and enjoyable days of the Jura Crest Trail. It packs a punch from the outset with the natural geological rock amphitheatre of the Creux du Van (1463m), south of Noiraigue, dramatically puncturing the landscape with a 160m vertical rock wall. The stage passes through the largest conservation area in the Canton Neuchâtel (25km²) and is home to arctic-alpine flowers, extensive forests and animals such as chamois and ibex. After gaining just over 650m within the first 5km, the route then passes over high alpine pastures, scarp ridgelines and finally summits Le Chasseron. The day ends in Sainte-Croix, but should you choose to shorten the stage, Chasseron and Les Cluds provide alternative finishing points.

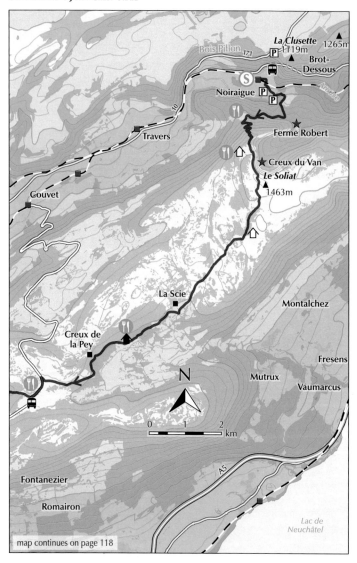

map continues on page 118

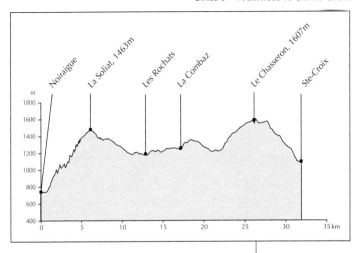

ABSINTHE

You may have noticed small bottles of green liqueur being offered and sold in buvettes, restaurants and shops on Stages 8 and 9. This is the potent and previously outlawed aperitif spirit of Absinthe which was invented in this part of the world. A local Swiss man, Daniel-Henri Dubied, stumbled across the recipe in 1797, but in 1830, due to high taxes, manufacturing was moved into neighbouring France. The liqueur was prohibited in Switzerland in 1910 and has only been made legal again in the last decade. The spirit is made of hardy wormwood leaves and flowers from the high Jura, mixed with fennel and lemon. A 35km absinthe trail can be followed, starting at Noiraigue and passing through the Doubs and on to Pontarlier in France.

Beginning the stage at **Noiraigue Gare**, turn right out of the station, heading in a south-east direction along Rue des Tilleuls followed by Rue de l'Areuse. Cross over the railway line and the River l'Areuse before arriving at the town overflow car park. Begin the ascent, passing Vers Chez Joly, before turning right onto a forest path for 1km, crossing over a gravel road, to reach a T-junction with a second gravel road. ▶

Turn left to take a short detour to the historic hut of Ferme Robert.

Ferme Robert, a mountain farmhouse at the base of the Creux du Van, was the last place that a bear was killed in the Jura in 1757. It is now an interpretation centre offering plenty of information about the area, as well as holding temporary exhibitions. The centre also hosts the traditional bear festival annually, at the end of August (www.ferme-robert.ch).

Turn right to continue along the Jura Crest Trail and follow it to **Restaurant des Oeuillons**, a popular buvette with the locals and a great place to rehydrate before a steep climb. From the restaurant, cross over the road and begin the ascent up a protected forest path, weaving through switchbacks for 2km, while climbing 350m in height. As you exit the forest, you continue to ascend for the **Creux du Van** to appear. Several paths have been formed in the area due to the number of visitors who climb to have their photo taken of them dangling their feet over the edge. ◄

Be careful when walking along the precipice, taking care with your footing.

The **Creux du Van** is a natural rock amphitheatre set among the rolling Jura landscape covering an area of 15km². Thick limestone deposits from the Jurassic period 160 million years ago helped form this breath-taking geological wonder. Within the 4km-long rock valley, 160m high cliffs offer spectacular views of the 1km-wide basin. An interpretation centre at the farmhouse Ferme Robert at the eastern end of the valley provides 3D videos and information on the geology of the area.

From the Creux du Van, head 1km south, passing the summit of **Le Soliat** (1463m) to your right. It is possible to stay overnight to enjoy a sunrise at the hotel and restaurant here.

Ferme Restaurant le Soliat: restaurant and hotel. Creux du Van, 2108 Couvet, tel +41 32 863 31 36, **www.lesoliat.ch**.

The dramatic cliffs of the Creux du Van

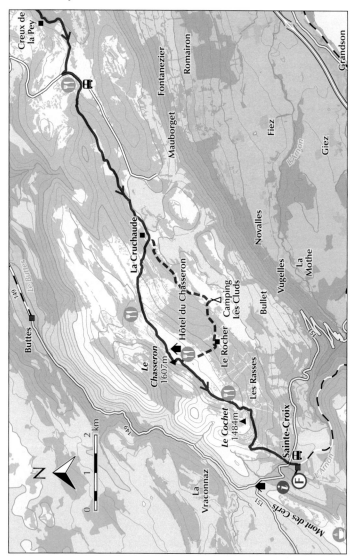

Descend through alpine pastures to **La Baronne** (1376m), another hostel and restaurant with road access. Cross over the road and continue the gradual 2km descent south-west, passing through gentle undulating pastures until you reach a tarmac mountain pass.

Turn left, following the road for 1.5km, passing the small dwelling **La Scie** (1172m) and layby on your right, before heading west on the footpath across alpine pastures with intermittent spruce trees. The path continues to gently descend through increasingly wooded undergrowth for 1.5km before joining the Chemin de la Montagnette to **Les Rochats**. The eatery is next door to an old military camp which has now been turned into a young offenders and detention centre. The area surrounding the restaurant still has a parade ground and tank driving area, along with plenty of signage warning you of military training.

From the restaurant, turn right and begin ascending a road into the forest. At the hairpin right-hand bend, turn left, heading south-west on a forest path, passing limestone outcrops before entering alpine pastures and a farm road at **Creux de la Pey** (1208m). Continue west to join the road, La Combe, at the bus stop.

Follow the road south to **Restaurant la Combaz** (1223m), a popular buvette with motorbikers who make use of the road separating the Val de Travers from Lac de Neuchâtel. ▸ Begin the gradual ascent behind the restaurant, following a footpath north-west for 500 metres to a spot height of 1303m on a small knoll before descending into a saddle to cross a small road. Continue ascending through woodland, heading in a south-west direction before contouring and navigating through alpine pastures and small farm buildings for 2.5km. The track continues south-west, opening onto wide grazing areas to the left and steep wooded hills to the right for 1.3km south-west to **La Cruchaude** (1223m), a summer farm building.

From the restaurant, the summit of Le Chasseron is a 2hr 30min hike away.

To overnight at Camping Les Cluds
There is an option to shorten the stage at La Cruchaude by continuing south-west for 3km to **Camping Les Cluds**.

The Jura Crest Trail carving its way through Norwegian spruce

Camping Les Cluds: campsite (part of the Camping Club Yvedon, 35 spaces for visitors, booking is mandatory). Les Cluds 20, 1453 Bullet, tel +41 24 454 14 40, ccy@campings-ccyverdon.ch, www.campings-ccyverdon.ch.

To reach the Jura Crest Trail following an overnight stay at the campsite, turn left to begin ascending through an alpine pasture followed by woodland up to a forest road for 200 metres. Cross over, bearing west, then south-west for 1km before reaching **Le Rocher** (1309m). Turn right, heading 300 metres north through a gradually ascending pasture, before continuing into the woods for a further 300 metres. As you exit the woodland, the prominent summit of Le Chasseron is 1km from this point and you ascend 230m to reach it.

Head north-west to begin the ascent to the summit of Le Chasseron, via a wooded track before opening out onto alpine pastures, up to **La Grandsonne Dessus** (1486m), a popular buvette open year round. From the buvette, continue south-west, ascending the ridgeline to the summit of **Le Chasseron** for panoramic views and an information board to help you distinguish key features and the surrounding area. ▸

The path from Camping Les Cluds rejoins the main route here.

> **Le Chasseron**, with a height of 1607m, is the fourteenth tallest mountain in the Jura. Its name is derived from 'la chasser', which in French means to hunt, chase or drive out something, a nod to its topography. Covering a large area, it has a southerly scarp slope and a northerly craggy cliff above a sunken valley.
>
> Due to the high snowfall in the area during the winter months, the southern side of the mountain is perfect for alpine skiing and is famous for its 80km of cross-country ski routes around Les Rasses. In the summer, Le Chasseron and its surrounds provide extensive hiking and mountain bike opportunities with 84km of trails and a number of buvettes offering local products and specialities.

> Hôtel du Chasseron: restaurant and hotel. 1452 Bullet, tel +41 24 454 23 88, **www.chasseron.ch**. Good accommodation, food and beverages are offered throughout the year.

The route continues 1.5km south-west along the ridgeline, over Petites Roches (1583m), where there are visible signs of winter sports activities such as skiing and snowshoeing. The 800m-length descent to Les Avattes, a buvette open year round, continues by passing over a saddle, by Refuge de la Casba, into a re-entrant. Join the gravel road to pass under the south-easterly slope of

Le Cochet (1484m), before circumnavigating the south-western flank of the peak, to the farmhouse Les Praises (1252m).

Turn left onto Rue La Casba and follow the road into **Sainte-Croix**.

SAINTE-CROIX

The mountain resort of Sainte-Croix is the starting place for many Jura adventures. With excellent transportation links connecting Yverdon-les-Bains in Switzerland, with the Doubs and Pontarlier in France, it sits high on the Col des Etroits, providing numerous opportunities to explore the outdoors. The most enjoyable route into the town is via the 15km narrow-gauge railway from Baulmes, passing through the picture-postcard station of Hotel de Trois-Villes before slowly ascending the precipice above the Gorges de Cooatanne.

The town has been known for its music boxes and musical instruments since work began crafting them in 1811 and you can visit several museums which demonstrate these masterpieces of precision engineering. There are also supermarkets and amenities, with Chambres d'Hôtes Grangette Bellevue providing reasonable accommodation just outside the town near the path to Vallorbe on Stage 10.

Chambres d'Hôtes Grangette Bellevue: bed and breakfast. Chemin de Grangette Bellevue 11, 1450 Sainte-Croix, tel +41 79 503 51 62, **www. grangette-bellevue.com**.

STAGE 10
Sainte-Croix to Vallorbe

Start point	Sainte-Croix (1086m)
Distance	24km
Total ascent	850m
Total descent	1100m
Grade	Easy
Time	7hr
Terrain	Categorised as a Wanderweg, the route predominantly follows wide, easy to navigate paths
High point	Chalet du Suchet (1489m)
Accommodation	Gîte Rural Bel Horizon (La Gittaz Dessus) 5km, Chalet de Grange-Neuve (north of Le Suchet) 8.5km, Camping Prè Sous Ville (Vallorbe) 24km, B&B Laffely (Vallorbe) 24km
Transport options	Train to Sainte-Croix from Yverdon-les-Bains (hourly); train from Vallorbe to Le Pont (hourly, 17min journey); train from Vallorbe to Lausanne (twice hourly, 50min); buses from Vallorbe to Yverdon-les-Bains (hourly)

The close proximity of this part of the Jura Crest Trail to the French border results in a stage dominated by its smuggling past, World War II defences and industry. The vast Pré-Giroud artillery fort is reached just before Vallorbe, strategically located with its arsenal aimed directly north through the valley towards France. The fortress was built from 1937 to 1941 and is a constant reminder of the past potential military invasions. The stage winds its way through gently rolling pastures, involving just one summit, Le Suchet (1588m), making it a pleasant day's walk.

Exit the train station to see a large hiking signpost next to a public toilets and water fountain. Turn left on the Avenue de la Gare, gently ascending towards the main town and shopping area. As you approach the Gendarmerie and Tourist Information Office, turn left and

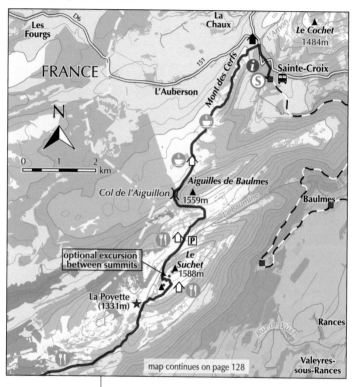

map continues on page 128

Before entering the tree line, take in the views of Sainte-Croix to the south and the summit cross of Les Rasses ski station to the east.

ascend the Rue de France, crossing several roads following onto a restricted non-motorised road to the main road (Avenue de Neuchâtel). Continue north for 300 metres before turning left onto a steep footpath beside a house, into an alpine meadow. ◄

Enter mixed woodland, turning left onto the paved road. Continue ascending for 200 metres onto an unpaved farm track. After the last house, follow this for 2km. From here the route begins a traverse of the Monts des Cerfs through alpine meadows and thickets of woodland, mostly Norwegian spruce alongside mature beech trees.

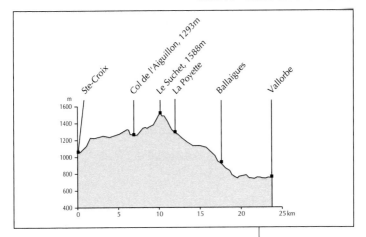

As you approach the quaint, typically Swiss hamlet of **La Gittax Dessous** (1239m), the track descends to a T-junction. Turn left onto the paved road, passing Café de la Gittaz with its outdoor seating and artwork on display of the surrounding rocks and local environment. Veer right passing through an open meadow for grazing to **La Gittaz Dessus** to Bel Horizon Chambres d'Hôtes. ▸

This point is 1hr 10min walking time from Sainte-Croix.

Bel Horizon Chambres d'Hôtes: hostel. La Gittaz Dessus 310, 1450 Sainte-Croix, tel +41 79 418 04 88, rjp.gebhard@gmail.com, **www. belhorizongiterural.ch**.

As you make your way towards to the base of the **Aiguilles de Baulmes** (1559m) you pass many remnants of Switzerland's military past and present. A number of bunkers, toblerone tank traps and fortresses can be seen in both obvious and more obscured locations as you descend to the rocky crags of **Col de l'Aiguillon**, a popular rock climbing location. ▸

The border with France is less than 500 metres away, to the west.

As you round the corner and head directly for a prominent bunker that appears to be in the middle of the road in the distance, the trees gradually open up to alpine

125

pastures either side, revealing an alpine cross signalling the highest point of the Aiguilles de Baulmes to the north (1553m). To the south, the heavily forested ridgeline of Le Suchet (1588m) opens up, revealing an undulating expanse of natural beauty. Turn off the road right, onto a footpath descending then ascending a re-entrant up to a paved road. Turn right, off the paved road to gradually ascend, passing a bunker, to **Chalet de Grange-Neuve Raymond Perriard** (1356m), a beautifully located auberge at the base of Le Suchet with commanding views up to the ridge and summit.

> Chalet de Grange-Neuve Raymond Perriard: mountain hut. Grange-Neuve, 1446 Baulmes, tel +41 23 459 11 81.

Turn onto the footpath through alpine pastures, gently ascending along the northern side of Le Suchet for 1km. The heavily forested rolling area of Joux de Lougne in France can be seen to the north, with the rocky outcrop of La Roche Marquée to the west and intermittent views south-west of Le Mont d'Or (1461m) behind in the distance. As you enter the tree line, the path becomes a difficult hiking path with tree roots and rocks protruding (red and yellow markers signifying a more mountainous route), steeply climbing, weaving its way to the Le Suchet plateau.

Pass over the saddle between the **Le Suchet summit** (1588m) and the cross (1553m), both of which are worthwhile to climb for the 360-degree views of the Alps, the Jura and the three lakes of Geneva, Neuchâtel and Lac du Joux. Drop down to **Chalet du Suchet** (1489m) before heading west, contouring around the base of the cross into alpine meadows. Descend the intermittently steep, uneven footpath to the toblerone tank traps at **La Poyette** (1331m).

> Throughout the Jura Crest Trail, you pass **remnants of military defences**. Switzerland remained neutral during World Wars I and II, although they ensured

The view from Dent de Vaulion looking back towards Sainte-Croix

they were heavily fortified and protected should any other country attempt to invade. The route between Sainte-Croix and Vallorbe passes numerous examples of military architecture, such as concrete bunkers, toblerone tank traps and old gun emplacements.

Cross over the road and take the hiking route signposted Vallorbe, descending a footpath through woodland, crossing over a paved road into an open pasture. Descend through the woods and yet more tank traps, to the farmhouse, La Languetine (1217m). Continue through mixed woodland for 1km, followed by open pastureland to **Chalet de La Tiole** (1142m), a traditional Swiss auberge serving food, with views of the prominent peak of Dent de Vaulion to the southwest and the spectacular geological escarpment of Le Mont d'Or to the west.

A fine view from the railway bridge towards Vallorbe and the Dents du Vaulion

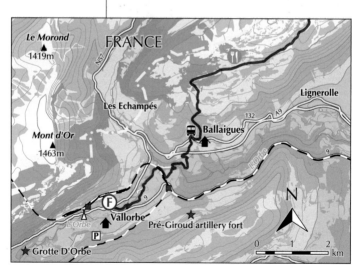

Continue across the paved road, onto a gravel farm track across the alpine pasture, into the woods. As you exit the woods, the track becomes paved, descending for 1km with views over the frontier town of Vallorbe. Turn right, off the paved road just after the farm Pré Magnin (1036m), onto a footpath through mixed woodland until you reach the town of **Ballaigues**. The track brings you out of the woods beside a house; turn right at the paved road, continuing down to the main road.

> The small town of **Ballaigues** provides an alternative finishing point for Stage 10, as it has extensive transport links to the surrounding area. By the bus stop on the main road, an information board provides detailed information about industry in the area, and in particular offers a small trail in the valley below. Just 400 metres west, in the wooded area of Chez Barrat, a historic Roman road track can be seen. This archaic route had wheel ruts cut into it and was used until the mid-19th century to guide carts transporting salt from Salins-les-Bains to larger cities such as Bern.

Cross the road to a viewpoint and information board, before turning right and descending the Grand-Rue, onto the single road, Les Grassis, through a line of defensive tank traps and over the bridge crossing the motorway (E23 linking Switzerland and France).

The road winds its way down a series of switchbacks, along farm roads. Attention needs to be paid due to limited signage, some of which is located on trees, and half the size of the usual markers because of smaller fence posts within the extensive farming land. Enter the track into the woods, being aware of the possibility of rock falls due to very crumbly limestone in the steep gorge.

Cross over the large dam (Barrage de L'Orbe), hidden in the depths of the gorge. ▶ Ascend the steep weaving track through woodland, which later develops into steps before the top. Turn right onto a gravel road through farmland where you are able to view the small but clearly

There is a particularly good view of the stunning architecture of the railway bridge upriver, which you later go under.

129

The River L'Orbe in full flow at Vallorbe

defined Swiss chalet with a large red cross hiding the fortress of **Pré-Giroud artillery fort** to the south.

Fort de Pré-Giroud, 2km south-east of the town of Vallorbe, is situated directly south of the Col de Jougne above the Franco-Suisse border crossing. The fort was built between 1937 and 1941 and provided a vantage point for any possible invasion. This large underground bunker and garrison housed up to 200 men during World War II.

The museum, shop and café are open in low season (mid-May to mid-October) at weekends 1030–1530 and in high season (July and August)

Wednesdays to Sundays. English tours by appointment in advance (Le Rosay, 1337 Vallorbe, tel +41 21 843 25 83, www.pre-giroud.ch).

Turn right and continue following the waymarked walking signs beside the railway track for 400 metres, passing the small power station before passing under the railway, through the first of the arches.

Follow the footpath along the south side of the River L'Orbe for 1km before entering the outskirts of the town of Vallorbe. As you walk to the end of Chemin des Plans-Praz, turn right onto Chemin de la Foulaz. Cross over the river by the footbridge, passing the Musée du Fer et du Chemin de Fer as you reach the centre of **Vallorbe**.

VALLORBE AND ENVIRONS

The River L'Orbe and the historic town centre of Vallorbe

The mountain town of Vallorbe developed during the Middle Ages due to its iron ore deposits and large supply of firewood, as well as being a frontier border town with France, thus making it a strategic hub for importing and exporting goods. The Musée du Fer et du Chemin de Fer is a museum dedicated to the railway and local industry near the town, providing an informative history of its past. Vallorbe has a large range of amenities, accommodation and transport links, offering extensive opportunities for onward travel.

Some 3km south-west of Vallorbe, at the source of

the River L'Orbe, is Grotte D'Orbe, a 3km underground cave system that can be explored. Discovered in 1974, the extensive galleries of stalagmite and stalactites are a worthwhile detour from the route (www.grottesdevallorbe.ch). With no direct transport links, the caves can be reached on foot via the river in around 15 minutes, or by taxi.

Further south-west, on the road to Le Pont, Jura Parc can be accessed by public bus or a 45-minute walk. Since 2001 the small park situated under the vertical rock cliffs of the Dent de Vaulion has re-homed wolves, bears and bisons in large enclosures similar to their natural habitats. Many of the animals have come from small zoos, enclosures or have been rescued. There is an informative walk (signposts in French) on elevated walkways (www.juraparc.ch).

Camping Prè Sous Ville: campsite in the centre of Vallorbe. Rue des Fontaines 8, 1337 Vallorbe, tel +41 21 843 23 09, camping@aapv.ch, **www.aapv.ch**.

B&B Laffely: bed and breakfast. Rue de l'Orbe 19, 1337 Vallorbe, tel +41 21 843 13 50, v.laffely@vonet.ch.

STAGE 11
Vallorbe to Col du Mollendruz

Start point	Vallorbe (788m)
Distance	12km; with Le Pont detour 17km
Total ascent	820m; with Le Pont detour 1110m
Total descent	380m; with Le Pont detour 880m
Grade	Easy to moderate
Time	4hr 30min; with Le Pont detour 6hr 50min
Terrain	The final ascent to the summit of Dent de Vaulion has some exposed parts and a small section that has fixed chains to assist with getting to the summit plateau. Categorised a Wanderweg
High point	Dent de Vaulion (1483m)
Accommodation	Village de Tipis (Les Ermitages) 12km, Chalet de la Breguettaz Sàrl (La Breguettaz) 12km, Hôtel de la Truite (Le Pont) 12km, Camping Lac du Joux (Rocheray, 7.5km from Le Pont) 19.5km
Transport options	Train from Vallorbe to Le Pont (hourly, 17min journey); train to Vallorbe from Lausanne (twice hourly, 50min journey); buses to Vallorbe from Yverdon-les-Bains (hourly); buses from Col du Mollendruz (twice daily in summer); Morges to Le Pont

The route from Vallorbe to the Dent de Vaulion epitomises typical Jura landscape. Leaving small picturesque Vallorbe, the trail winds its way up through mixed woodland to crest a ridge up to an antenna. The summit on a clear day provides 360-degree panoramic views of rolling alpine pastures interspersed with evergreen trees, Lac du Joux, the largest lake in the Jura massif, the forested border with France, as well as the high peaks of the Savoie Alps.

The area is famed for its watch making and its cheese industry. Vacherin Mont d'Or AOP is a soft cheese that comes in a distinctive round box made of local spruce to give it a distinctive woody flavour, available between the months of August to March. Many local buvettes and restaurants across the region serve the baked cheese, which is infused with garlic and white wine and served with boiled potatoes.

The stage also offers the opportunity to detour off the Jura Crest Trail to visit the small lakeside village of Le Pont, which is well worth the extra kilometres.

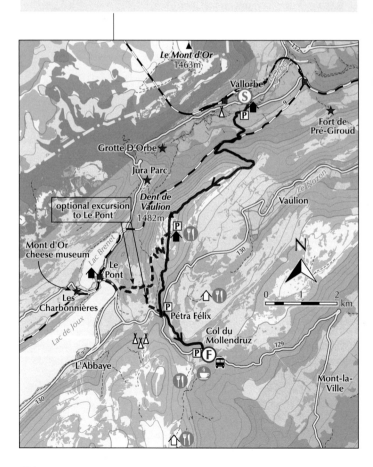

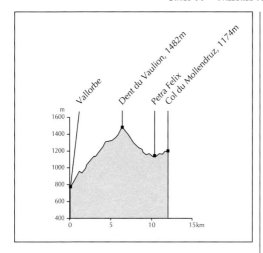

From the centre of **Vallorbe** return to the River L'Orbe and cross the main bridge south and follow the flow upstream until you reach the road bridge. From here, take the footpath south-west, passing the ice skating rink, up to the Rue de l'Orbe. Follow the paved road past Les Revinnox, ascending gradually as you head south, taking the left-hand fork at spot height 776m.

The road intersects grazing pastures, continuing into mixed woodland before turning 90 degrees, heading west-south-west. ▶

As the road turns south, opening a clear view of Vallorbe to the north, follow the left-hand turn onto a rocky, steep and wide footpath. The rocks are loose underfoot and it is not very easy to ascend.

Passing under the railway through an arch, take the left footpath. It is not marked; beware of the right-hand defined and well-trodden route signposted with yellow diamonds. The path ascends steeply, swerving in an easterly direction, following the railway line for approximately 100 metres on a track before contouring around, into woodland. At the end of the path, it joins a paved single road. Turn right, gradually ascending for 100

As you begin to ascend, beech and Norwegian spruce trees become dominant alongside many shrubs and undergrowth.

Commune refuge overlooking Mont d'Or

metres until the road forms a hard-standing gravel forest road. Stay on the main path, keeping right until you reach a refuge (approximately 900 metres) on the right-hand side. The refuge has several picnic tables and a fire pit outside, as well as providing shelter from the rain. There is an information board with a map and a selection of endangered species of plants to look out for. The views across the valley extend as far as Ballaigues and over the border into France and the Mont d'Or plateau, a perfect place to stop, rehydrate and have a snack.

Continue up the gravel road until you meet a four-way junction. Turn left heading in an east-south-east direction, again ascending the forest road. From here, the path is marked with intermittent yellow signposts. After approximately 800 metres, having passed through a small crossroads for the mountain biking tracks, another four-way junction appears. Take the track straight ahead, which has a short descent of 10 metres before gradually ascending through mixed woodland. The climb gradually increases through the forest as you approach a large rock.

Due to the path being eroded and not well maintained, exposed limestone and tree roots far outweigh sensible foot placements. The track narrows and weaves its way to the foot of the crag, steepening as you near the top of the tree line. ▶

The track opens onto a wide expanse of meadows and grazing pastures with views across the valley from Romainmôtier in the south-east to the Col du Mollendruz in the south-west.

Turn right onto the paved road from Vaulion, ascending gradually towards La Mâche (1204m), a summer farm dwelling. As you near the farmhouse, 20 metres before reaching it, pass through the gate on the right side of the road, joining a farm track, heading in a south-easterly direction. The track is not very defined or walked very often so take care not to stray off route. Pass a small refuge on the right and continue to a turnstile gate where you are directed north-west to a small copse, before joining another long, narrow strip of grazing land between woodland. At the end of the clearing, pass through a turnstile before heading into mixed woodland on a wide forest track. After several hundred metres the route narrows before opening to a junction with a forest road. Take the eroded, wooded footpath to the right, ascending steeply for a short period, onto a narrow track that appears to be a knife-edge, with a very steep drop on the right-hand side. ▶

This is one of the best parts of the trek with amazing views across the valley towards Mont d'Or in France, as well as beautiful forested, craggy valleys and small lakes below. The path turns west-north-west, ascending steeply over eroded ground with minimum vegetation and exposed rocks. Pass through the turnstile, heading straight up the steep slabs of limestone, before reaching the fence line. You will now be in full view of the tall telecommunications tower that sits on top of the summit, **Dent de Vaulion** (1483m). The stunning views of the surrounding mountains of the Jura, as well as the Alps, are spectacular. An information board on top of the summit provides information regarding the heights of peaks visible, as well as distances from your location. ▶

This section of track is very narrow and care should be taken if carrying heavy rucksacks.

The path has exposed limestone and tree roots that make it difficult under foot, especially when wet.

You should leave the route here if you wish to overnight in Le Pont (see below).

*Mont d'Or cheese,
a local speciality*

Following a 730m height gain from the start of the route, descend south through alpine meadows with low intermittent rocky outcrops towards the **Buvette de la Dent de Vaulion** (1410m). The buvette serves typical mountain food and drink, and is the perfect place to stop and experience the local cheese, Vacherin Mont d'Or.

Continue south on the paved single road for 25 metres until it sweeps to the left, forming a hairpin bend, and take the footpath to the right passing what seems like a World War II concrete bunker, which is actually the underground reservoir housing. The footpath descends gradually through alpine meadows with isolated trees, passing a refuge (1360m) on the left.

Pass through the turnstile to join a track into the mixed woodland for 100 metres before it opens up, joining onto a wider forest road (stay to the right-hand side), through predominantly deciduous woodland, formed mostly of beech trees. Contour around a natural spur, before leaving the forest road to join a track that descends south into the woodland.

The footpath follows an undulating series of short, steep ascents and descents for approximately 400 metres, along an eroded track exposing sharp limestone rocks and slippery tree trunks, before joining a gravel, rocky forest road. Turn right, descending the path for approximately 70 metres before reaching the **Pétra Félix car park**. Some 100 metres before the end of the track, the forest path passes between toblerone tank traps, part of the National Redoubt Plan left after World War II. ▸

The detour via Le Pont rejoins the main route at the car park.

On reaching the car park, you meet the main road over the Col du Mollendruz, linking La Côte to the Vallée de Joux region. Turn left, walking to the corner of the road junction with the pass. An alternative choice of accommodation can be located just 1.5km south-west of the car park, in the form of large traditional tipis.

Village de Tipis: campsite, Rue du Moulin, 1344 L'Abbaye, tel +44 78 739 16 82, info@tipis.ch, **www.tipis.ch**. A northerly aspect slope with views across Lac du Joux and the Risoux Forest, this is basic, remote camping in ready-to-use tipis all with open fires to cook on, both inside and outside the tent.

Cross over the minor road, signposted Yverdon and Vaulion, taking the narrow paved road that runs parallel, descending into the forest. Follow the track, descending until you pass over a cattle grid across the road. ▸

La Breguettaz, a remote buvette and hotel, can be reached by taking the footpath north for 2km.

Chalet de la Breguettaz Sàrl: hotel and restaurant. La Breguettaz, 1148 Mont-la-Ville, tel +41 21 843 29 60, labreguettaz@bluewin.ch, **www.labreguettaz.ch**.

Continue straight ahead, veering right slightly, through a meadow until you pass over a second cattle grid separating the grazing pastures and woodland. After

The car park is intermittently serviced during the summer months by a local postal bus, check www.sbb.ch.

100 metres the road becomes a gravel forest track, continue gently ascending, turning right upon meeting a path from the left. The forest track opens onto a small clearing, again meeting with the **Col du Mollendruz**. Continue heading south-east, following the track through the woodland for 100 metres until you drop into the Col du Mollendruz main **car park**. ◄

The Auberge du Mollendruz at the col has been shut for several seasons now, therefore do not expect accommodation or services. There are basic amenities at the Nordic Sport, located at the start of Stage 12, by the car park on the main road where you will find a shop, toilet and small café.

To visit Le Pont

Le Pont, at the western end of Lac du Joux, is a typical Jura mountain village

From the summit of **Dent de Vaulion**, head in a southerly direction, towards Buvette de la Dent de Vaulion (1410m). Take the footpath, west, passing the hut toilets, through a drystone wall, across the alpine meadow and ski chalet on your right. The track becomes more obvious

Having fun on Lac du Joux with Le Pont and the Dents du Vaulion in the background

as you begin to descend through isolated trees, small copses and alpine pastures until a gravel road appears. Pass the summer farmhouse, La Petite Dent (1348m), on your right then commence the descent of switchbacks all the way to another alpine farmhouse, La Dent (1194m). As can be seen by the eroded paths, some hikers have taken shorter routes in descent, cutting off the corners. ▶

It is better if you stay on the path provided, minimising erosion on this very popular hike, ascending and descending the same route.

The paved road follows a re-entrant in a southerly direction for 600 metres before gradually turning east to a four-way junction. Take the paved road straight ahead, dropping down to the right to join a footpath, cutting off the hairpin corner on the paved road. Pass through a metal turnstile and descend meadow and grazing land before passing through a gap in a drystone wall. The area can get quite marshy and wet underfoot so stay to the path as there is a small grid bridge to take you over a stream before passing through another turnstile to return to a paved road.

Turn left onto the paved road, descending as you travel between two steep craggy mountainsides. Pass between two concrete blocks either side of the road (used to shut the road when military operations take place), leading to revealing views of **Lac du Joux**. Descend steeply to the right onto a footpath that passes beside a house. Cross over the paved minor road, again heading towards the lake, passing the boulangerie to reach **Le Pont**.

LE PONT

The small lakeside town of Le Pont offers a picture-postcard setting, a treat for the eyes after a day's hike. The small, pebbled beaches offer swimming, sailing and paddling during the summer months. Lac du Joux is the highest lake of the Jura (1000m), and it frequently freezes over in the winter to provide a large outdoor ice skating rink enjoyed by locals. Le Pont is accessible by train, via Vallorbe, or by post bus over one of the many cols found in the Jura from the shores of Lake Geneva. Several campsites are located beside the lake, as well as a hotel and B&B accommodation. There is also a range of amenities including a convenience store, crêperie, several bars and restaurants.

North-west of Le Pont is a smaller lake, Lac Brenet, which has a circular walk around the perimeter with stunning views of the north face of the Dent de Vaulion.

Hôtel de la Truite: hotel and restaurant. Rue de la Poste 4, 1342 Le Pont, tel +41 21 841 17 71, **www.hoteltruite.com**.

Camping Lac du Joux: campsite (9km south-west of Le Pont, on the train line between Le Pont and Le Chenit). Le Rocheray 37, 1347 Le Chenit, tel +41 21 845 51 74, **www.camping-club-vaudois.ch**. (See Stage 12 map.)

To rejoin the Jura Crest Trail at the Pétra Félix car park, from the boulangerie at Le Pont ascend gradually away from the lake, crossing over a paved minor road to join a track through a re-entrant, heading east. A steep concrete ramp tops the footpath and leads you onto a paved concrete road. Turn left onto the road and follow it around to the right into a steep-sided ravine. Pass through a concrete military roadblock either side of the road and look out for the bunker sat on the steep mountainside up to your right. ◄ Pass through a second military roadblock either side of the road before pastureland opens up on

This area is scattered with reminders of the events of World War II.

A dramatic view of Dent de Vaulion from Lac Brenet

the right-hand side. Follow the paved road around to the left for a further 200 metres where a notice board informs you of some local history surrounding the famous German writer and poet Goethe who passed through in 1779.

VACHERIN MONT D'OR

Vacherin Mont d'Or, a local dairy speciality of the Vallée de Joux area, is available between 15 August and 15 March annually. Mont d'Or received an AOP (controlled origin appellation) in 2003, protecting its origin, of the village of Les Charbonnières, 1km south-west of Le Pont. The soft cheese, enclosed in a wooden case produced using local trees, has a distinct smoky flavour and has been a favourite of the Jura since the early 19th century. The cheese dish is wrapped in foil, pierced with garlic cloves and soaked in white wine before being baked in the oven for 45 minutes. The Vacherin Mont d'Or museum at Les Charbonnières provides a detailed insight into the history of the cheese (www.vacherin-le-pelerin.ch).

Take the turnstile to the right to access the footpath across the meadow, crossing a small grid bridge and drystone wall before gently ascending to the paved road. Follow the footpath to the left of the road, avoiding the hairpin bend, before taking the road to the right at the crossroads. Pass over a cattle grid, heading directly south for 500 metres until the road turns right. Take the footpath to the left, passing through a farm gate to enter a large field. Begin the gentle ascent in a south-easterly direction before passing through a turnstile separating pasture land and forest, that brings you onto a drivable gravel forest track. Ascend the track, passing through a line of toblerone tank traps until you reach the **Pétra Félix car park**.

STAGE 12
Col du Mollendruz to Col du Marchairuz

Start point	Col du Mollendruz (1174m)
Distance	17km
Total ascent	950m
Total descent	580m
Grade	Easy
Time	5hr 30min
Terrain	The route predominantly follows wide, easy to navigate footpaths through pastures. Mont Tendre, a high ridgeline with little cover, can leave the hiker exposed in bad weather
High point	Mont Tendre (1679m)
Accommodation	Cabane du Cunay (5.5km north-east Col du Marchairuz) 11.5km, Hôtel du Marchairuz (Marchairuz) 17km
Transport options	Buses serving Col du Mollendruz (twice daily in summer) travel between Le Pont and Morges; buses serving Col du Marchairuz (May to October, weekends only) travel between Le Brassus to Allaman

In good conditions, the crossing of Tendre massif promises to be one of the main highlights of the Jura Crest Trail, providing panoramic views of Mont Blanc and the Savoie Alps. The trail starts and ends at two main crossing points, enabling easy access to and from the section, as well as summiting the highest peak in the Swiss Jura range, Mont Tendre.

The southern end of the Jura trail is steeped in history, providing interesting additional routes off the main track to explore, and there is an optional extension to summit Châtel (1420m), a southerly viewpoint with farmland and vineyards stretching down towards Lake Geneva.

From the western car park at **Col du Mollendruz** follow the gravel farm road past the **Nordic Hut**, heading in a

145

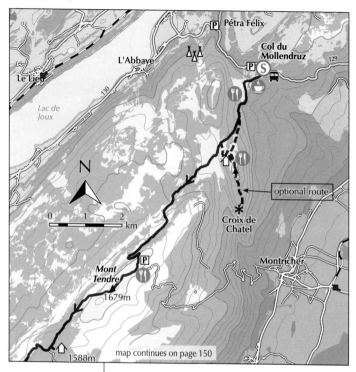

south-west direction for 300 metres, through open meadows. This first part of the route can be hard to follow due to trails for shorter hikes in the area, as well as winter signage for the snowshoe season. At the left-hand turn in the road into the forest, bear right, off the road onto a track. Continuing west-south-west for a further 350 metres, you meet a small gravel farm road heading south, passing **Chalet du Mollendruz**, a buvette providing very good local food and hot drinks. Turn right onto a track at the small crossroads to ascend a wooded path for 400 metres before reaching a series of tank traps. Turn right onto a tarmac road (Combe de la Neige) to begin a gentle ascent up a valley surrounded by trees.

PASSEURS AND SMUGGLING

The border with France lies parallel to the trail, 10km north-west and it is scattered with tank traps. Also known as 'toblerones', these army defences are dispersed throughout the Jura, a reminder of past conflict. Another relic from the past can be seen in the forest across the valley, north of Lac du Joux. During World War II *passeurs* (smugglers) transported Jews, prisoners of war and spies through the dense Risoux Forest, over the Jura to the safety of Switzerland. Evidence of the heroic locals can be seen by the monument to commemorate the *passeurs* at the northern end of Lac du Joux. Follow the Col du Mollendruz road north, through Le Pont. The obelisk is located in front of the hotel, by the lake.

To visit the summit of Châtel

▶ A worthwhile detour to summit Châtel can be taken after 50 metres on the Combe de la Neige. Turn left off the road onto a small footpath to begin a reasonably steep ascent up a ridgeline through the forest. After 400 metres it opens up onto alpine pasture before passing **Buvette de Châtel** (1148m, 1hr 40min).

This adds 2km and 120m in height.

> Buvette de Châtel: bar and restaurant. 1148 L'Isle, tel +44 21 841 12 26, open May to September daily.

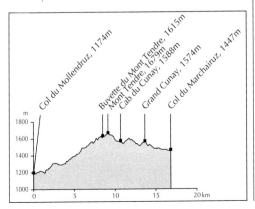

Continue heading south for a further 500 metres where you will discover a large alpine crucifix, the **Croix de Châtel**, at spot height 1420m, giving 180-degree panoramic views atop a craggy escarpment across Lake Geneva to the French Haute Savoie Alps. To return to the Jura Crest Trail, re-trace your steps back to Buvette de Châtel, turning left to descend the tarmac access road to the buvette, to join with Combe de la Neige, 1km west of where you accessed the road originally.

The detour to the viewpoint at Châtel rejoins the Jura Crest Trail here.

Continue ascending through the valley passing a picturesque typical Swiss chalet on the right, and the road access to the buvette at Châtel on your left. ◀ Remain on the road for a further 100 metres before joining and descending the tarmac road south-west across the alpine pasture for 600 metres to spot height 1292m. Turn right at the crossroads, onto a gravel farm road through a mixture of scattered woodland and open pastures west-south-west for 1.5km to spot height 1417m. The track turns left onto a wooded path to begin to ascend, then contour the ridge to Chalet de Pierre, a farm building for summer

The view west from Mont Tendre

grazing. Turn left to join a gravel farm road to continue ascending through woodland to the top of the ridgeline to again reveal a stunning panoramic view of the lake and the Alps, before heading down to **Buvette du Mont Tendre** (1615m, 2hr).

> Buvette du Mont Tendre: bar and restaurant. Route du Mont Tendre, 1147 Montricher, tel +41 78 739 59 47, claudecrottaz@hotmail.ch, **www.buvette-mont-tendre.ch**, open May to September.

To reach the highest peak in the Swiss Jura follow the single rocky path south-west from the buvette to the prominent triangular summit post of **Mont Tendre** (1679m). ▸

You may see danger signs warning you not to pick up ordnance or explosive devices – the Swiss army train on the southern flank of the mountain, 6km away, at certain times of the year.

ALPINE FLOWERS

Mont Tendre is a very special site for alpine flowers. In June 1966 the Cercle Vaudois de Botanique discovered 198 plant species within the vicinity of the summit. Because of the limestone escarpment, as well as areas of dense woodland, this section of the route is home to a wonderful array of exciting plants.

One flower in particular stands out. The *Gentiana lutea*, otherwise known as the Giant Yellow Gentian, can grow up to 1m in height and comprises a large head of yellow flowers clustered together like grapes. It can grow up to 50 years and weighs 7kg when fully matured. The roots of the plant are important in this area of the Jura, extending to 1m in length. Locals macerate and then distil the roots to make a botanical aperitif, enjoyed with local cheeses.

All along the route, a range of flowers such as gentians, bellflowers (campanula) and crocus, alongside established trees such as white fir (*Albies alba*), red fir (*Piecea abies*) and common juniper (*Juniperus communis*) can be seen.

The route is easier to follow from here, as there are not as many access points or walkers along the ridge to the Col du Marchairuz. Begin the descent from Tendre, on a single rocky track passing Chalet de Yens on the north-west side of the summit. Continue contouring along the northern side of the ridgeline, through strip pastures interspersed with Norwegian spruce. After 1.5km of undulating Jura terrain you reach a communication antenna and installation camouflaged among the trees.

Some 200 metres to the south of the installation, the mountain hut **Cabane du Cunay** (1588m, 4hr) appears sitting atop a vantage point with stunning views across the lake and the Alps.

Cabane du Cunay: CAS basic mountain hut with dormitory. 1145 Bière, tel +41 21 845 55 87, **www. cas-valdejoux.ch** (sleeping bag liner required, bring own food, book in advance).

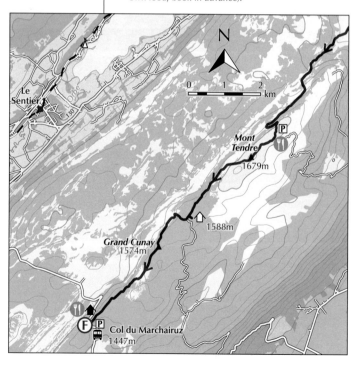

Sunflowers on the slopes of the Jura

In 2010 the Swiss Army attempted to place a 25m-high **antenna** on the summit of Mont Tendre, much to the disgust of the residents of the canton of Vaud. After several protests from the World Wildlife Fund, Pro Natura and local nature lovers, it was placed atop of the small knoll at spot height 1609m, just north of Cabane du Cunay instead, leaving Mont Tendre to remain a tender, gentle rolling peak.

Rejoining the path, follow route 5 north-west on the tarmac road, down through the pasture to Chalet des Combes. Turn left, continuing south-west on a track to the intermittently exposed limestone **Grand Cunay** (1574m). The undulating path along the ridgeline continues through pastures filled with a vast range of alpine flowers throughout the spring and summer season, including many species of gentians, campanula and crocus. Pass over the crossroad at Monts de Bière Derrière, continuing a further 500 metres through grazing pasture, before entering mixed woodland for the 1.2km to the **Col du Marchairuz**. Upon reaching the pass be sure to cross at an appropriate place – do not be drawn north towards the hotel, due to a blind corner. Instead turn left (southwards), descending the road slightly, before crossing to reach the hotel and the end of Stage 12.

COL DU MARCHAIRUZ

The Col du Marchairuz (1447m) connects Lake Geneva with Lac du Joux. The medieval hilltop town of Aubonne, 15km south-east, provides a post bus service throughout the summer months, linking the mountain town of Saint-George with the col, then north to Le Brassus. This prominent route has been a significant transport link since as early as the 13th century when settlements on Lake Geneva needed to be connected with Lac du Joux. Check the timetable on www.sbb.ch for specific timings as they can change from season to season.

From the hotel, where you can find a detailed map outside the main entrance to the hotel, you can follow a series of marked information trails, for example, a 9km geology trail or a smaller flower route. More information can be found on the Parc Jurassien Vaudois website (www.parcjuravaudois.ch).

Hôtel du Marchairuz: bar, restaurant and hotel. Place du Village 8, 1188 Saint-George, tel +41 21 845 25 30, info@hotel-marchairuz.ch, **www.hotel-marchairuz.ch**, closed Mondays but open all year round.

STAGE 13
Col du Marchairuz to Saint-Cergue

Start point	Col du Marchairuz (1447m)
Distance	17km
Total ascent	480m
Total descent	900m
Grade	Easy
Time	5hr
Terrain	Categorised as a Wanderweg, the wide, easy to navigate route has limited ascent due to mostly contouring along a wide ridgeline
High point	Crêt de la Neuve (1493m)
Accommodation	Cabane de Rochefort (3km north of Saint-Cergue) 20km, Hôtel Restaurant de la Poste (Saint-Cergue) 17km, Camping des Cheseaux (Saint-Cergue) 17km
Transport options	Buses serving Col du Marchairuz (May to October, weekends only) travel between Le Brassus to Allaman; trains between La Cure and Nyon (twice hourly, throughout the day)
Note	Beware of cattle on this section of the route, especially if there are young calves present

The traverse of the Balcon du Leman from the Col du Marchairuz offers some of the best views of Lake Geneva and the Savoie Alps of France, including Mont Blanc in the distance. The col has linked the Vallée de Joux, an area famed for watch making, with Lake Geneva since the 13th century. The trail follows the ridgeline, passing traditional stone walling to separate alpine pastures scattered with Norwegian spruce and alpine summer farming huts, as well as passing directly through ancient monastic ruins. This area has been a protected nature reserve since 1972.

A highly recommended detour towards the end of the stage is to the Fromagerie des Fruitières de Nyon, where you can observe traditional cheese-making in an alpine chalet. On arrival in Saint-Cergue, there are accommodation options to choose from, as well as public transport to Lake Geneva and into France should you wish to explore further afield.

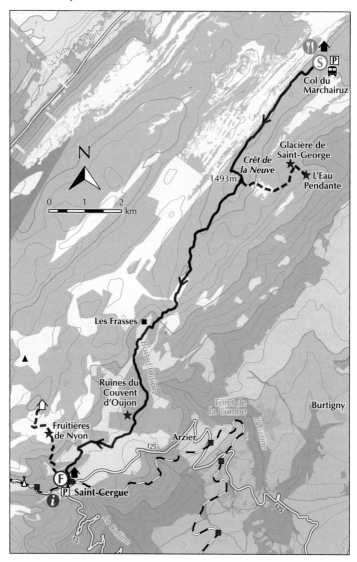

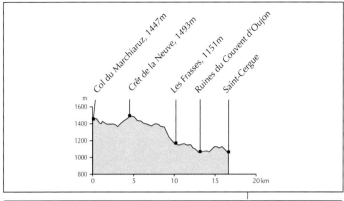

PARC JURA VAUDOIS AND LAC DU JOUX

With over 523km of trails for hikers, mountain bikers, cross-country skiers and snowshoers, the Parc Jura Vaudois, the largest nature park in the canton of Vaud (over 100km²), offers a range of outdoor adventure activities within a variety of environments. Lac du Joux sits at an altitude of 1000m at the northern end of the park. Being nestled within a high valley, it affords its own microclimate, leading to natural ice skating in the winter months and a range of water sport activities in the summer months, such as sailing, paddling and windsurfing.

The area around Saint-George and all the way to Saint-Cergue has clear signs of forestry, as well as other conservation projects. A large area of the Jura was deforested during the 18th and 19th centuries for industry, and charcoal in particular. In recent years it has been protected and re-planted following conscious efforts by the local community. There is an information centre located at Saint-George (www.parcjuravaudois.ch).

From the hotel at the **Col du Marchairuz** take the route in front of the terrace and wooden outbuilding, to ascend a short track into the woods. ▸ The first 800 metres of the trail goes through woodland on a rocky path which can become quite slippery when wet. The route continues south-west, along the Bois du Marchairuz, a narrow strip of grazing pasture, lined with stone walls, surrounded by mixed woodland.

Due to the proximity of the inn, many tracks weave through this area; be sure to follow the yellow diamond hiking path signs on trees.

155

A view over France from the summit of Mont Tendre

The area is famed for its wild **mushrooms**. A tradition involving collecting a variety of species using big baskets is upheld by locals who make use of the access road along the Combe des Amburnex, running parallel to the Jura Crest Trail, 500 metres north.

You can hear the cattle before seeing them generally because of the traditional bells that identify each individual cow.

Continue south-west along the path, passing through small drystone wall crossing points, just wide enough to slide through sideways in order to contain the grazing cattle that reside on the hill during the summer months, before descending to the Jura winter farms. ◄

As you approach La Neuve (1442m), a large traditional Jura summer farm building surrounded by open pastures, beware of the large number of cattle congregating here waiting to be fed. Pass through the gate to the south of the farm building and turn left, heading east, ascending a gravel farm track. After 200 metres, pass through a metal turnstile to continue ascending the track through woodland up to the viewpoint of **Crêt de la Neuve** (1493m), a perfect spot for a rest break.

The summit of **Crêt de la Neuve** hosts an observation deck, a circular drystone wall that helps with protecting hikers from the occasional cold blasts, with views across Lake Geneva and the Alps. A 4.5m traditional alpine cross was erected in 2011 and stands alongside a flagpole that adorns the Swiss ensign over the summer months.

CATTLE ON THE JURA

Throughout the Jura Crest Trail you will encounter cows during the summer months, as nearly 600,000 milking cows are brought to the high pastures. As soon as local herdsmen and women feel the temperature rising and consider the grazing ready for the season, they walk their cattle to the high alpine pastures to graze on the grasses and wildflowers; the floral and herbal plants provide added flavour to locally produced cheese. As the weather cools during the autumn, the herdsmen and women, alongside many of the local population, celebrate the end of the season through the annual event of *désalpes* (French) or *alpabfahrt* (German). Usually taking place at weekends, the cows are decorated in colourful floral garlands, sprigs of Norwegian spruce and large cattle bells that date back many years and are paraded through the streets. The cow which produced the most milk during the season is proclaimed the 'queen' cow and to identify her, she wears the largest bell.

To visit the Glacière de Saint-George

▸ From the viewpoint at **Crêt de la Neuve**, descend the steep open pasture following the worn track onto the footpath 100 metres below the summit. Continue descending through woodland until you reach a paved farm road (1399m). Follow the road past Petit Pré de Rolle, a summer farm dwelling, leading through an expansive pasture with sporadic Norwegian spruces.

The trip is 2.5km in length with 250m height gain and takes 1hr 30min.

After 1km, as the road descends into woodland and around a hairpin bend, turn left onto the footpath. Continue on the footpath heading north-east to the cave.

Glacière de Saint-George is located in a large subterranean cave set 22m underground. You can access the unmanned, remote cave via two wooden ladders between May and November to see the glacier, which was once used to supply ice to local brasseries.

Another attraction further along the route in a north-easterly direction is a waterfall. Continue on the footpath to the junction with a wide forest path (1249m), before turning right and contouring around to **L'Eau Pendante**. Views open up across the Combe de la Menthe towards Saint-George and Bière, two mountain villages with public transport access to the Jura.

At **L'Eau Pendante**, the waterfall cascades down the rockface from a mysterious origin to a religious monument and natural water tank made of larch for visitors to enjoy and rehydrate from. In days gone by it was used by the horsemen transporting ice.

Return to the Crêt de la Neuve via the same route you descended.

From Crêt de la Neuve, continue along the undulating ridgeline, along strip pastures, ancient drystone walls and established firs, passing Perroude de Marchissy, a buvette occasionally open during summer months (plan in advance and do not expect services).

The trail turns left, heading south onto a tarmac access road for several hundred metres before continuing through pastures and mixed woodland, passing **Les Frasses** (1151m), an alpine farming hut. From this point, the trail continues to descend through mixed woodland (Bois d'Oujon) with several vantage points, including ready-made fire pits built by locals who regularly enjoy a sunset picnic, overlooking Mont Blanc. As you approach the **Ruines du Couvent d'Oujon** signposts can be misleading due to the many hiking routes in the area.

The **Abbey of Oujon** was founded in 1306 and has exchanged hands due to several conflicts over the centuries. The abbey has been well preserved and

Looking towards Mont Blanc from the ridge descending into Saint-Cergue

provides information (not in English) on the history of the building and area. You may see signposts for the Chemin Spirituel d'Oujon guided walk. There are 12 information points starting and finishing in Arzier, a village several kilometres away.

Continuing on, the wooded trail opens out onto expansive farming pastures, intermittently crossing paved roads before descending into the mountain village of Saint-Cergue. The trail leads you onto the paved Chemin des Couteaux that joins Les Cheseaux Dessus, the access road to the railway station in **Saint-Cergue**.

SAINT-CERGUE

The mountain village of Saint-Cergue lies in a high col (1041m) separating two prominent ridgelines of the south-western part of the Jura. Originally developed as an alpine spa in the 19th century, it became even more popular following the 1916 construction of a narrow-gauge railway from the shores of Lake Geneva. The 'little red train' is a scenic train journey through vineyards, mountain ravines and on to the high pastures, linking Nyon in Switzerland with La Cure in France.

A popular hiking spot in summer and winter (on snowshoes), the area offers extensive opportunities for outdoor adventure activities. During the summer months numerous hiking and mountain biking routes can be completed within the 100km² area of woodland and meadows of the Parc Jura Vaudois. With its own alpine ski lift in the village, winter activities including night time skiing, are also offered.

Hôtel Restaurant de la Poste: bar, restaurant and hotel (18 beds and Wi-Fi). Route de Nyon 5, 1264 Saint-Cergue, tel +41 22 360 12 12, **www.delaposte.ch**.

Camping des Cheseaux: campsite. Route du Télésiège 12, 1262 Saint-Cergue, tel +41 22 360 18 98, **www.camping-club-vaudois.ch**.

To overnight at the Cabane Rochefort

A worthwhile option is to overnight in a remote cabin, Cabane Rochefort, 4km north of Saint-Cergue. It can only be accessed on foot, taking 1hr 15min. Follow the signposts for Fruitières de Nyon (1333m) from Saint-Cergue train station, heading north for 200 metres onto the Route de Basse Ruche north-west of the village. Following the footpath, ascending wooded, steep terrain for 1km to a large plateau of alpine pastures. On route, you pass Chalet Devant, where the **Fruitières de Nyon** (1333m) is located.

Fruitières de Nyon is a traditional alpine fromagerie allowing visitors the opportunity to watch the cheese-making process and learn about traditional methods. You can also sample a variety of cheeses produced locally: gruyere, raclette and the speciality of the chalet, tonneau d'alpage, a semi-hard cheese, which is matured for 8–10 months. It is

well worth the trip and opens from 0700-1200 and 0400-0700 daily during the months of May and September, tel +41 22 364 52 60.

View over Mont Blanc from the Jura Plateau (photo: Jonathan Williams)

Join the road, bearing north-north-west for 300 metres to meet a junction. Take the footpath, gradually ascending in a westerly direction for 200 metres, before turning right to head north-east for 500 metres to reach the **Cabane Rochefort** (1418m).

Cabane Rochefort: CAS mountain hut (31 beds). 1273 Arzier-Le Muids, **www.cas-la-dole.ch**. A simple mountain hut with bunk beds, a stove and basic toilets, alongside a stunning view over the French alps. Booking in advance is mandatory.

To travel back to Saint-Cergue, retrace your steps.

STAGE 14
Saint-Cergue to Nyon

Start point	Saint-Cergue (1042m)
Distance	26km
Total ascent	800m
Total descent	1450m
Grade	Easy to moderate, with one section of hard
Time	6hr 45min
Terrain	A longer stage with conditions becoming moderate to hard upon approach to the summit of La Dôle where the path narrows and handrails the north of the precipice
High point	La Dôle (1677m)
Accommodation	Domaine de Bois-Bougy (Nyon) 24km, Nyon Hostel (Nyon) 27km, Camping Rolle (Rolle, 11km north-east of Nyon)
Transport options	Trains between La Cure and Nyon (twice hourly, throughout the day); regular onward regional trains available throughout Switzerland from Nyon: Geneva is 16 minutes away

The final stage continues through Parc Jura Vaudois with this protected area of outstanding natural beauty continuing to deliver in the scenery stakes. Starting in the picturesque mountain village of Saint-Cergue with its many amenities such as restaurants, hotels, ski resorts and good public transport, this stage epitomises Switzerland in miniature. The hiking path gradually climbs through alpine pastures before the final scarp slope climb to the top of La Dôle, a geological natural amphitheatre, before descending through spruce forests, famous Vaud vineyards and arable pastures to the historic town of Nyon on the shores of Lake Geneva.

From **Saint-Cergue** railway station head south-west along Rue de la Gare, onto Route d'Arzier, passing a range of convenience stores, restaurants and hotels. After going straight over the roundabout, turn right onto Chemin

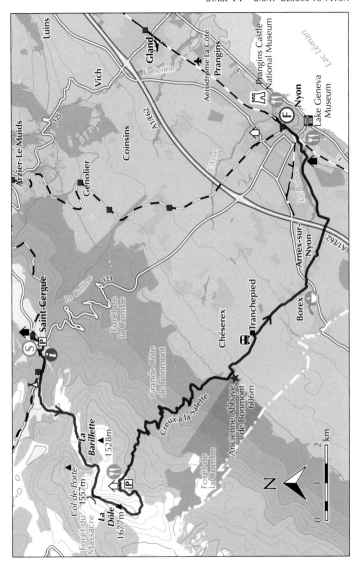

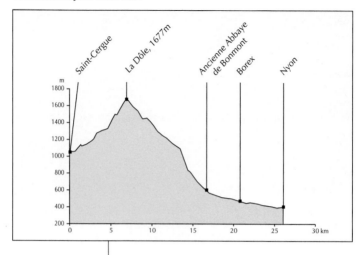

Jean-Jacques Rousseau. Follow the trail along a paved road past the ski lifts and the Déchetterie (recycling point) of the local commune. Continue north-west, pass **Camping des Cheseaux**, a well-priced campsite.

Turn left, 100 metres after the campsite, to cross an open pasture for grazing, before joining the Route du Télésiège, heading south, past the commune hut and car park – a favourite local start point for hikes in La Dôle area.

Continue due south, gradually ascending through grazing pastures before accessing the Route de Vuarne, a paved road heading west up a valley with high escarpments either side. The path continues as a track shortly after spot height 1320m, gradually getting steeper as it ascends to the col (1486m) between Pointe de-Poêle Chaud (1628m) and La Barillete (1528m).

Turn right at the crossroads of four footpaths, passing Chalet des Apprentis, on a narrow track, ascending to **Col de Porte** (1557m). The Ski Club du Nyon own the little mountain hut at the col, a perfect location to stop, have a break and enjoy the stunning views across the Alps to the south-east and the French Jura to the north-west, overlooking the Forêt du Massacre and the French ski resort of Les Rousses. ▶

The trail up to the summit is confusing, not least due to grazing cattle, wandering tourists and plentiful ski routes in the area, leading to erosion and many paths being created. Pass through the stile, turning left to continue on the footpath, being sure to contour around, and not ascend, the ridgeline. The official footpath, and the one described here, passes to the northern side, underneath the ridgeline, staying away from the steep drop into the Les Creux.

La Dôle is aloft at 1677m, with the drama of a 250m steep precipice: 'There are no words to describe the grandeur and the beauty of this spectacle' J.W. Goethe, the famous German poet and writer, wrote in 1779 as he passed the peak on his way to Geneva. This rocky, Jurassic outstanding natural feature, sitting above Nyon, offers a vantage point with panoramic views to the far west of Switzerland including Lake Geneva and as far as the 140m-high Jet d'Eau water fountain in the centre of the Geneva.

Forêt du Massacre is named after a 1535 clash between the Savoyards and 600 Italian mercenaries flighting over the city of Geneva.

A dramatic view from the summit of La Dôle looking east towards the summit La Barillette

The geological amphitheatre and golf-ball summit of La Dôle

The 'golf-ball' summit station can be easily distinguished for many miles around. The radar facility, alongside MétéoSuisse weather forecasting unit, is part of Skyguide's air traffic control for Western Switzerland and adjoining foreign airspace. A panoramic mountain display can be seen from the viewpoint, detailing all the surrounding mountains and points of interest across Lake Geneva.

Continue descending, being sure not to be drawn left, to the steeper, craggy headwall of Les Creux. Again, because of a large number of cattle and chamois populating the area, in particular during the summer months, many paths have been trodden. Keep to the painted yellow diamonds on the rocks, descending below the summit of La Dôle, to reach **Chalet de la Dôle**.

Chalet de la Dôle: restaurant (irregular opening hours). Famille Golaz, 1276 Gingins, tel +41 79 656 82 38. This buvette is favoured by locals due to the views and easy access to La Dôle, alongside good mountain food and refreshments.

Begin to descend the paved road, heading south-east until you reach a junction (1422m) with the road to La Barilette. Cross over the road, descending a path through the forest for 1km, crossing the road twice before rejoining the road for 200 metres. On the apex of the bend, take the footpath left, running parallel with the gravel forest road, before again descending down the **Creux à la Salette**, a natural hollow, through mixed woodland, to Le Bauloz (1132m), a forestry hut.

Continue south-east, descending the **Grande Côte de Bonmont**, a forested area above the ancient abbey, before rejoining the paved road for 600 metres. On the hairpin bend, turn right, descending a steep path for 2km, crossing over the road three times before arriving at **Ancienne Abbaye de Bonmont** (606m), a golf course and country club.

VINEYARDS OF VAUD

The vineyards of La Côte and the canton of Vaud are famous for their sweet, refreshing white wines thanks to the warm climate, low altitude and favourable aspect. The Route du Vignoble de La Côte, a path celebrating the vineyards of the area, starts at Versoix near Geneva, passing through Nyon and on to Morges. Many vineyards and 'caves' of the region are open to visitors: you can sample their delights or even plan a visit to one of many annual wine festivals, such as the famous celebration at Fechy in September (www.vinsfechy.ch).

Follow the Route du Stand for 500 metres, before turning left onto a footpath through the woods for 250 metres. Turn left onto the paved road for 200 metres before turning right onto Route d'Angelot, continuing south-east for 1km to a farmyard (**Tranchepied**). Continue south-east passing through the farm until it reaches the main road, Route de Crassier. Cross over the main road, to join the Route de Tranchepied for 750 metres to enter the outskirts of the village of **Borex**. Follow the road for a further 750 metres which brings you to a road junction and the main hub of the village.

A small tearoom, **La Ferme**, can be found on the main road, 50 metres right of the junction.

La Ferme: restaurant and tearoom. Route de Crassier 8, 1277 Borex, tel +41 22 367 0067, **www. restaurant-la-ferme.ch**.

Go straight over the roundabout, following the Route de Borex through **Arnex-sur-Nyon**, onto the Route Menant Au Bois-du-Nant. After navigating the overpass bridge of the motorway (A1/E62), bear left until you meet the main road, Route de Crans. Cross over the road, onto Chemin des Trois-Chenes, following it for just over 1km, turning left onto a footpath descending over the bridge of the river, **Le Boiron**. Rejoining a paved road, turn right onto Chemin du Lignolet, up to the main street, Route de Clémenty. Pass over the railway line via the road bridge, then turn left onto Avenue Reverdil onto Place de la Gare. South-east of the train station is the old town and beyond that the lakeside where bars and restaurants will provide you with celebratory refreshments.

A view enjoyed while descending La Dôle looking south-east towards Lake Geneva

NYON

Nyon Chateau

The charming town of Nyon and its castle have stood securely since the 13th century, a permanent fixture during periods of change: the Romans inhabited the area in ancient times, the ruler of Bern dominated the town in the 16th century and more recently it was a significant position during World War II when fortifications were built all over this part of the Jura to stop any advancements from the Germans. The town has many significant sights and so it makes a good final destination. Prangins Castle to the east of Nyon is set in a very attractive building and is home to the Swiss National Museum which celebrates 18th- and 19th-century Switzerland on display (www.nationalmuseum.ch). The Museum of Lake Geneva is in the centre of Nyon, near the port and details the history of the lake, its origins, shipping, fishing and industry (www.museeduleman.ch). Due to lying on the regional SBB line, Nyon easily connects Switzerland nationally and internationally, through the extensive public transport system of the country.

For those who wish to celebrate the end of the 310km journey along the Jura Crest Trail, Nyon offers a vast range of restaurants and bars, most of which are found 500m south-east of the train station in the old town and along the lakeside. Restaurant de la Plage, located on the edge of Lac Leman, 500m west of the marina, offers a large range of local specialities from the lake. More central, the Rue de Rive offers a selection of bars, pubs, restaurants and cafes to choose from: Brasserie Le Rive offers a view of the lake, good food and a selection of drinks, and the Fishermens Pub provides an array of beverages and international bar snacks.

If you have time at the end of your journey, or have a keen interest in military history, an optional excursion from Bassins railway station, which can be reached on the 'little red train' from Nyon, is highly recommended. The 17km easy Promenthouse Line Hiking Trail, which descends 460m and takes about five hours, is strewn with tank traps. This area of defence that lies between the foot of the Jura and Lake Geneva was called the Promenthouse Line, also known as the Toblerone Line, and signposts along the route give an in-depth account of what Switzerland was like during World War II.

Domaine de Bois-Bougy: B&B. Chemin de Bois-Bougy 4, 1260 Nyon, tel +41 22 361 34 52, barbarabernegger@romandie.com, **www.bnb.ch/897**. Wi-Fi is available.

Nyon Hostel: hostel. Chemin des Plantaz 47, 1260 Nyon, tel +41 22 888 12 60; info@nyonhostel.ch, **www.nyonhostel.ch**.

Camping Rolle: campsite on Lake Geneva. Chemin des Vernes, 1180 Rolle, tel +41 21 825 12 39, camping@rolle.ch, **www.campingrolle.ch**.

Restaurant de la Plage, Route de Genève 12, 1260 Nyon, tel +41 22 362 61 01, info@laplagedenyon.ch.

Fishermen's Pub, Rue de Rive 37, Nyon 1260, tel +41 22 362 84 10, **www.thefishermenspub.com**.

Brasserie Le Rive, Rue de Rive 15, 1260 Nyon, tel +41 22 552 20 82, **www.hotel-le-rive.ch**.

APPENDIX A
Accommodation

Stage 1
Jugendherberge Baden (hostel)
Kanalstrasse 7
5400 Baden
tel +41 56 221 67 36
www.youthhostel.ch

Jugendherberge Brugg (hostel)
Im Hof 11
5200 Brugg
tel +41 56 441 10 20
www.youthhostel.ch

Gasthof Bären Bözberg (hostel,
campsite and restaurant)
Neustalden 6
5225 Bözberg
tel +41 56 441 15 65
www.baeren-boezberg.ch

Stage 2
Waldgasthaus Chalet Saalhöhe
(hotel and restaurant)
Saalhöhe 156
4468 Kienberg
tel +41 62 844 10 14
www.chalet-saalhoehe.ch

Naturfreundehaus Schafmatt
(bunkhouse and restaurant)
4494 Oltingen
tel +41 78 803 40 98
www.schafmatt.ch

Hotel Froburg (hotel and restaurant)
Froburgstrasse 262
4634 Wisen
tel +41 62 293 29 78
www.restaurant-froburg.ch

Gästezimmer Salzmann
(bed and breakfast)
Oberdorf 2
4633 Hauenstein
tel +41 62 293 24 55
ly.salzmann@bluewin.ch

Stage 3
Restaurant Chilchli
(hotel and restaurant)
Bärenwil 193
4438 Langenbruck
tel +41 62 390 11 13
www.chilchli.ch

Genussgaasthaus Tiefmatt
(hotel and restaurant)
Tiefmattstrasse 109,
4718 Holderbank
tel +41 62 390 20 60
www.tiefmatt.ch

Stage 4
Berggasthof Schwengimatt
(restaurant and hostel)
Schwengimatt 50
4710 Balsthal
tel +41 62 391 11 49
www.schwengimatt.ch

Stage 5
Berggasthof Untergrenchenberg
(B&B and restaurant)
Untergrenchenberg
2540 Grenchen
tel +41 32 652 16 43
www.untergrenchenberg.ch

Restaurant Stierenberg
(restaurant and hotel)
Grenchenberg
2540 Grenchen
tel +41 32 652 16 44
www.grenchenberge.ch/grenchenberge/
stierenberg

Swiss Hostel Lago Lodge
(hostel, off route)
Uferweg 5
2560 Nidau
tel +41 32 331 37 32
www.lagolodge.ch

Hôtel La Truite (hotel and restaurant,
off route)
Rue de la Reuchentte 3
Pery 2603
tel +41 32 485 14 10
www.hotellatruite.ch

Stage 6
Cabane du Jura (mountain hut)
2534 Orvin
www.sac-biel.ch

Bison Ranch (camping, off route)
Les Colisses 101
2534 Les Pres d'Orvin
tel +41 32 322 00 24
www.bisonranch.ch

Stage 7
Chalet du Mont d'Amin
2054 Chézard-Saint-Martin
tel +41 032 853 24 26
www.cas-chauxdefonds.ch

Hôtel de la Vue-des-Alpes
(hotel and restaurant)
Vue des Alpes
2052 Fontaines

tel +41 32 854 20 20
www.vue-des-alpes.ch

Stage 8
CAS Fiottet
(Sommartel Section mountain hut)
fiottet@cas-sommartel.ch

Hôtel de la Tourne (hotel and restaurant)
La Tourne
2019 Rochefort
tel +41 32 855 11 50
resto.latourne@gmail.com

Hôtel Grill Restaurant
(hotel and restaurant)
Crêt de l'Anneau 1
2105 Travers
tel +41 32 863 11 11

Stage 9
Ferme Restaurant le Soliat
(hotel and restaurant)
Creux du Van
2108 Couvet
tel +41 32 863 31 36
www.lesoliat.ch

Camping Les Cluds (campsite)
Les Cluds 20
1453 Bullet
tel +41 24 454 14 40
www.campings-ccyverdon.ch

Hôtel du Chasseron
(restaurant and hotel)
1452 Bullet
tel +41 24 454 23 88
www.chasseron.ch

Chambres d'Hôtes Grangette Bellevue
(bed and breakfast)
Chemin de Grangette Bellevue 11
1450 Sainte-Croix
tel +41 79 503 51 62
www.grangette-bellevue.com

Stage 10
Gîte Rural Bel Horizon (hostel)
La Gittaz Dessus 310
1450 Sainte-Croix
tel +41 79 418 04 88
www.belhorizongiterural.ch

Chalet de Grange-Neuve Raymond
Perriard (mountain hut)
Grange-Neuve
1446 Baulmes
tel +41 23 459 11 81

Camping Prè Sous Ville (campsite)
Rue des Fontaines 8
1337 Vallorbe
tel +41 21 843 23 09
www.aapv.ch

B&B Laffely (bed and breakfast)
Rue de l'Orbe 19
1337 Vallorbe
tel +41 21 843 13 50

Stage 11
Village de Tipis (campsite, off route)
Rue du Moulin
1344 L'Abbaye
tel +44 78 739 16 82
www.tipis.ch

Chalet de la Breguettaz Sàrl
(hotel and restaurant)
La Breguettaz
1148 Mont-la-Ville
tel +41 21 843 29 60
www.labreguettaz.ch

Hôtel de la Truite (hotel and restaurant)
Rue de la Poste 4
1342 Le Pont
tel +41 21 841 17 71
www.hoteltruite.com

Camping Lac du Joux (campsite)
(off route)
Le Rocheray 37
1347 Le Chenit
tel +41 21 845 51 74
www.camping-club-vaudois.ch

Stage 12
Cabane du Cunay (CAS basic mountain
hut with dormitory)
1145 Bière
tel +41 21 845 55 87
www.cas-valdejoux.ch

Hôtel du Marchairuz
(bar, restaurant and hotel)
Place du Village 8
1188 Saint-George
tel +41 21 845 25 30
www.hotel-marchairuz.ch

Stage 13
Hôtel Restaurant de la Poste
(bar, restaurant and hotel)
Route de Nyon 5
1264 Saint-Cergue
tel +41 22 360 12 12
www.delaposte.ch

Camping des Cheseaux (campsite)
Route du Télésiège 12
1262 Saint-Cergue
tel +41 22 360 18 98
www.camping-club-vaudois.ch

Cabane Rochefort CAS
(mountain hut, off route)
1273 Arzier-Le Muids
www.cas-la-dole.ch

Stage 14
Domaine de Bois-Bougy (B&B)
Chemin de Bois-Bougy 4
1260 Nyon
tel +41 22 361 34 52
www.bnb.ch/897

Nyon Hostel (hostel)
Chemin des Plantaz 47
1260 Nyon
tel +41 22 888 12 60
www.nyonhostel.ch

Camping Rolle (campsite, off route)
Chemin des Vernes
1180 Rolle
tel +41 21 825 12 39
www.campingrolle.ch

APPENDIX B

Useful contacts

Tourist information
Swiss Alpine Club
www.sac-cas.ch/en.html

UK
Switzerland Travel Centre Ltd
1st Floor
30 Bedford Street
London WC2E 9ED
United Kingdom
tel +44 20 7 420 4934
Sales@stc.co.uk
https://switzerlandtravelcentre.co.uk

Switzerland
Zurich Main Station
Bahnhofpl
8001
Zurich
Switzerland
tel +41 44 215 40 00
info@zuerich.com
www.zuerich.com

Info Baden
Bahnhofplatz 1
5400 Baden
tel +41 56 200 87 87
info@baden.ch
www.baden.ch

Brugg Regio
Badenstrasse 13
5200 Brugg AG
tel +41 56 560 50 00
info@bruggregio.ch
www.bruggregio.ch

Tourismus Biel/Bienne Seeland
Bahnhofplatz
Postfach 1261
2501 Biel/Bienne
tel +41 32 329 84 84
info@biel-seeland.ch
www.biel-seeland.ch

Office du Tourisme de Sainte-Croix/
Les Rasses
Rue Neuve 10
1450 Sainte-Croix
tel +41 24 455 41 42
ot@sainte-croix.ch
www.sainte-croix-les-rasses-tourisme.ch

Office du Tourisme de Vallorbe
Grandes-Forges 11
Case Postale 90
1337 Vallorbe
tel +41 21 843 25 83
contact@vallorbe-tourisme.ch
www.vallorbe-tourisme.ch

Office du Tourisme de St-Cergue
Place Sy-Vieuxville 3
1264 Saint-Cergue
tel +41 22 360 13 14
www.region-du-leman.ch

Geneva Tourist Information Office
Rue du Mont-Blanc 18
1202 Geneva
Switzerland
tel +41 22 909 70 00
info@geneve.com
www.geneve.com

Nyon Region Tourism
Avenue Viollier 8
1260 Nyon
Switzerland
tel +41 22 365 66 00
info@nrt.ch
www.lacote-tourisme.ch

Maps

Stanfords London
12–14 Long Acre
Covent Garden
London WC2E 9LP
tel +44 20 7836 1321
sales@stanfords.co.uk
www.stanfords.co.uk

Stanfords Bristol
29 Corn Street
Bristol BS1 1HT
United Kingdom
tel +44 117 929 9966
Bristol@stanfords.co.uk
www.stanfords.co.uk

The Map Shop
15 High Street
Uptown upon Severn
Worcester WR8 0HJ
tel +44 1684 593146
themapshop@btinternet.com
www.themapshop.co.uk

Swiss Federal Office of Topography
www.swisstopo.admin.ch

Switzerland Mobility
(Swiss online mapping resource)
www.schweizmobil.ch

Specialist mountain activities insurance

British Mountaineering Council (BMC)
The Old Church
177–179 Burton Road
West Didsbury
Manchester M20 2BB
tel +44 161 445 6111
insure@thebmc.co.uk
www.thebmc.co.uk

Snowcard Insurance Services
Lower Boddington
Daventry
Northamptonshire NN11 6XZ
tel +44 1702 427273
ai@ageas.co.uk
www.snowcard.co.uk

World Nomads
21/680 George Street
Sydney
NSW 2000
Australia
tel +44 330 660 0549
infoGBR@worldnomads.com

Austrian Alpine Club UK
Unit 43 Glenmore Business Park
Blackhill Road
Poole BH16 6NL
United Kingdom
tel +44 1929 556870
aac.office@aacuk.org.uk
www.aacuk.org.uk

Transport

By air
British Airways
www.britishairways.com

Easyjet
www.easyjet.com

SWISS
www.swiss.com

Edelweiss air
www.flyedelweiss.com

Flybe
www.flybe.com

Jet2
www.jet2.com

TUI
www.tui.co.uk

Skyscanner (easy to use cheap flight finder)
www.skyscanner.net

eBookers (flight and accommodation finder)
www.ebookers.com

By rail

Swiss Federal Railways (SBB/CFF/FFS)
(the Swiss national rail network where
you can locate train timetables,
purchase tickets and travelcards)
www.sbb.ch

Eurostar (London to Paris train travel tickets)
www.eurostar.com

French National Railway Company
(SNCF)
(Paris to Switzerland train travel tickets)
www.sncf.com

Weather

MeteoBlue
(makes use of a selection of local
weather forecasts to give an average)
www.meteoblue.com

MeteoSwiss
(the Swiss national weather forecast
website)
www.meteoswiss.admin.ch

Mountain Forecast
(mountain weather website, although
not very detailed for the Jura mountains)
www.mountain-forecast.com

Emergencies

Emergency number
tel 112

REGA (mountain rescue)
tel 1414

APPENDIX C
Glossary

Greeting and pleasantries

English	German	French
Hello	Hallo	Bonjour
How are you?	Wie gehts?	Comment allez-vous?
My name is…	Ich heiße…	Mon nom est…
Goodbye	Auf Wiedersehen	Au revoir
Where is the…?	Wo ist der…?	Où est le…?

Useful mountain terms

English	German	French
Accommodation	Unterkunft	Hébergement
Drinking water	Trinkwasser	Eau potable
Left	Links	À gauche
Right	Rechts	À droite
Straight	Geradeaus	Tout droit
North	Norden	Nord
East	Osten	Est
South	Süden	Sud
West	Westen	Ouest
Cave	Höhle	Grotte
Col	Scharte	Col
Compass	Kompass	Boussole
Danger!	Achtung!	Danger!
High	Hoch	Haut
Lake	See	Lac

English	German	French
Ridge	*Grat*	*Arête*
Rock	*Fels/Felsen*	*Rocher*
Steep	*Steil*	*Raide*

Emergency terms

English	German	French
There has been an accident	*Es gab einen Unfall*	*Il y a eu un accident*
My GPS coordinates are…	*Meine GPS Koordinaten sind*	*Mes coordonnées GPS sont*
The victim is unconscious	*Das Opfer ist bewusstlos*	*La victime est inconsciente*
The victim isn't breathing	*Das Opfer atmet nicht*	*La victime ne respire pas*
I need a rescue helicopter	*Ich brauche einen Rettungshubschrauber*	*J'ai besoin d'un hélicoptère de sauvetage*
Head	*Kopf*	*Tête*
Neck	*Nacken*	*Cou*
Arm	*Arm*	*Bras*
Knee	*Knie*	*Genou*
Leg	*Bein*	*Jambe*
Ankle	*Knöchel*	*Cheville*

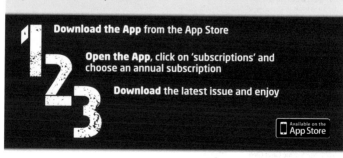

LISTING OF CICERONE GUIDES

SCOTLAND
Backpacker's Britain:
  Northern Scotland
Ben Nevis and Glen Coe
Cycling in the Hebrides
Great Mountain Days in Scotland
Mountain Biking in Southern and
  Central Scotland
Mountain Biking in West and North
  West Scotland
Not the West Highland Way
Scotland
Scotland's Best Small Mountains
Scotland's Mountain Ridges
Scrambles in Lochaber
The Ayrshire and Arran
  Coastal Paths
The Border Country
The Cape Wrath Trail
The Great Glen Way
The Great Glen Way Map Booklet
The Hebridean Way
The Hebrides
The Isle of Mull
The Isle of Skye
The Skye Trail
The Southern Upland Way
The Speyside Way
The Speyside Way Map Booklet
The West Highland Way
Walking Highland Perthshire
Walking in Scotland's Far North
Walking in the Angus Glens
Walking in the Cairngorms
Walking in the Ochils, Campsie
  Fells and Lomond Hills
Walking in the Pentland Hills
Walking in the Southern Uplands
Walking in Torridon
Walking Loch Lomond and
  the Trossachs
Walking on Arran
Walking on Harris and Lewis
Walking on Rum and the
  Small Isles
Walking on the Orkney and
  Shetland Isles
Walking on Uist and Barra
Walking the Corbetts
  Vol 1 South of the Great Glen
Walking the Corbetts
  Vol 2 North of the Great Glen
Walking the Galloway Hills
Walking the Munros
  Vol 1 – Southern, Central and
  Western Highlands

Walking the Munros
  Vol 2 – Northern Highlands and
  the Cairngorms
West Highland Way Map Booklet
Winter Climbs Ben Nevis and
  Glen Coe
Winter Climbs in the Cairngorms

NORTHERN ENGLAND TRAILS
Hadrian's Wall Path
Hadrian's Wall Path Map Booklet
Pennine Way Map Booklet
The Coast to Coast Map Booklet
The Coast to Coast Walk
The Dales Way
The Dales Way Map Booklet
The Pennine Way

LAKE DISTRICT
Cycling in the Lake District
Great Mountain Days in the
  Lake District
Lake District Winter Climbs
Lake District: High Level and
  Fell Walks
Lake District: Low Level and
  Lake Walks
Mountain Biking in the Lake District
Scrambles in the Lake District
  – North
Scrambles in the Lake District
  – South
Short Walks in Lakeland Books 1–3
The Cumbria Way
Tour of the Lake District
Trail and Fell Running in the
  Lake District

NORTH WEST ENGLAND
AND THE ISLE OF MAN
Cycling the Pennine Bridleway
Cycling the Way of the Roses
Isle of Man Coastal Path
The Lancashire Cycleway
The Lune Valley and Howgills
The Ribble Way
Walking in Cumbria's Eden Valley
Walking in Lancashire
Walking in the Forest of Bowland
  and Pendle
Walking on the Isle of Man
Walking on the West
  Pennine Moors
Walks in Lancashire Witch Country
Walks in Ribble Country
Walks in Silverdale and Arnside

NORTH EAST ENGLAND,
YORKSHIRE DALES AND
PENNINES
Cycling in the Yorkshire Dales
Great Mountain Days in
  the Pennines
Mountain Biking in the
  Yorkshire Dales
South Pennine Walks
St Oswald's Way and
  St Cuthbert's Way
The Cleveland Way and the
  Yorkshire Wolds Way
The Cleveland Way Map Booklet
The North York Moors
The Reivers Way
The Teesdale Way
Walking in County Durham
Walking in Northumberland
Walking in the North Pennines
Walking in the Yorkshire Dales:
  North and East
Walking in the Yorkshire Dales:
  South and West
Walks in Dales Country
Walks in the Yorkshire Dales

WALES AND WELSH BORDERS
Cycling Lôn Las Cymru
Glyndwr's Way
Great Mountain Days in Snowdonia
Hillwalking in Shropshire
Hillwalking in Wales – Vols 1 & 2
Mountain Walking in Snowdonia
Offa's Dyke Map Booklet
Offa's Dyke Path
Pembrokeshire Coast Path
  Map Booklet
Ridges of Snowdonia
Scrambles in Snowdonia
The Ascent of Snowdon
The Ceredigion and Snowdonia
  Coast Paths
The Pembrokeshire Coast Path
The Severn Way
The Snowdonia Way
The Wales Coast Path
The Wye Valley Walk
Walking in Carmarthenshire
Walking in Pembrokeshire
Walking in the Forest of Dean
Walking in the South Wales Valleys
Walking in the Wye Valley
Walking on the Brecon Beacons
Walking on the Gower
Welsh Winter Climbs

For full information on all our guides, books and eBooks, visit our website:
www.cicerone.co.uk

Walking – Trekking – Mountaineering – Climbing – Cycling

Over 40 years, Cicerone have built up an outstanding collection of over 300 guides, inspiring all sorts of amazing adventures.

Every guide comes from extensive exploration and research by our expert authors, all with a passion for their subjects. They are frequently praised, endorsed and used by clubs, instructors and outdoor organisations.

All our titles can now be bought as **e-books**, **ePubs** and **Kindle** files and we also have an online magazine – **Cicerone Extra** – with features to help cyclists, climbers, walkers and trekkers choose their next adventure, at home or abroad.

Our website shows any **new information** we've had in since a book was published. Please do let us know if you find anything has changed, so that we can publish the latest details. On our **website** you'll also find great ideas and lots of detailed information about what's inside every guide and you can buy **individual routes** from many of them online.

It's easy to keep in touch with what's going on at Cicerone by getting our monthly **free e-newsletter**, which is full of offers, competitions, up-to-date information and topical articles. You can subscribe on our home page and also follow us on **Facebook** and **Twitter** or dip into our **blog**.

Cicerone – the very best guides for exploring the world.

CICERONE

Juniper House, Murley Moss, Oxenholme Road, Kendal, Cumbria LA9 7RL
Tel: 015395 62069 info@cicerone.co.uk
www.cicerone.co.uk